Evidence, Argument, and Persuasion in the Policy Process

Evidence, Argument and Persuasion in the Policy Process

Giandomenico Majone

Yale University Press
New Haven and London

Set in Baskerville type by Rainsford Type,
Danbury, Connecticut.
Printed in the United States of America by
BookCrafters, Inc., Chelsea, Michigan.

Library of Congress Cataloging-in-Publication Data
Majone, Giandomenico.
Evidence, argument, and persuasion in the policy process
Giandomenico Majone.
p.   cm.
Bibliography: p.
Includes index.
ISBN 0-300-04159-4 (alk. paper)
1. Policy sciences.   2. Persuasion (Rhetoric)   I. Title.
H97.M36   1989
361.6'1—dc19   88–21677
                                                  CIP

The paper in this book meets the guidelines for
permanence and durability of the Committee on
Production Guidelines for Book Longevity of the
Council on Library Resources.

10   9   8   7   6   5   4   3   2

*To Eleonore, Andrea, and Giorgio
who know everything there is to know
about the art of persuasion*

Contents

Preface

I started working on the ideas that eventually led to this book more than a decade ago. At that time the notion that (rhetoric,) the ancient art of persuasive discourse, had anything to do with professional policy analysis seemed to many colleagues to be not only far-fetched but also dangerous. These colleagues feared that to question the image of analysts as technicians supplying data for the preexisting preferences of policymakers would threaten the position of policy analysis as an academic discipline and undermine efforts to introduce rationality and efficiency in the confused world of policy-making.

This was not, of course, my intention. Having been trained as a Bayesian statistician, I felt that the attempt to enlarge the scope of policy analysis to include such common practices as persuasion, rationalization, and advocacy—thus bringing these practices under rational control—was rather similar to the efforts of students of subjective probability to extend the range of application of statistical and probabilistic reasoning beyond the traditional domain of repetitive events and mass phenomena.

The occasional acrimony of the debate between Bayesian and traditional statisticians should not obscure the fact that the classical theory is completed rather than contradicted by the new developments based on the concepts of utility and subjective probability. In the same way, to attempt to reconstruct policy analysis on the basis of rhetorical categories—to view the analyst as a producer of arguments, capable of distinguishing between good and bad rhetoric, rather than as a "number cruncher"—is not to deny the usefulness of the traditional analytic skills. Modeling, mathematical programming, simulation, cost-benefit analysis, and decision analysis will always remain important tools. However, if the purpose of policy analysis is not simply to find out what is a good or satisfactory policy but to ensure that the policy will actually be chosen and implemented, the traditional skills are not sufficient. The analyst must also learn rhetorical and dialectic skills—the ability to define a problem according to various points of view, to draw an argument from many different sources, to adapt the argument to the audience, and to educate public opinion.

The centuries-old tradition of humanistic disciplines, from history and literary criticism to moral philosophy and law, proves that argumentative skills can be taught and learned. Thus, if the crucial argumentative function of policy analysis is neglected in university departments and schools of public policy, this is due less to a lack of suitable models than to serious misconceptions about the role of reason in human affairs and about the nature of the "scientific method." When mathematicians acknowledge that mathematics is not the antithesis of rhetoric and that mathematics may sometimes be rhetorical just as rhetoric may sometimes be mathematical, as Philip J. Davis and Reuben Hersh argue in their book *Descartes' Dream*, it should not be left to policy analysts to fight the last battles of positivism.

The fact that work on this book has so often been interrupted by other commitments has turned out to be a blessing in disguise, since it has given me the opportunity to exchange ideas with a large number of colleagues and students at a variety of institutions on both sides of the Atlantic: the International Institute for Applied Systems Analysis in Laxenburg, Austria; the Center for Interdisciplinary Research of the University of Bielefeld; the Wissenschaftszentrum in Berlin; the Russell Sage Foundation in New York; the Institution for Social and Policy Studies of Yale

University; the John F. Kennedy School of Government of Harvard University; and the European University Institute in Florence.

It is impossible to list here the names of all the colleagues and students whose comments have greatly improved earlier drafts. I would like to mention at least Michael Barzelay, Tom Burns, William C. Clark, Robert Lane, Charles Lindblom, Theodore Marmor, Hugh Miser, Mark Moore, Richard Nelson, Richard Neustadt, E. S. Quade, Jerry Ravetz, Robert Reich, and Aaron Wildavsky. I thank them all for their critical attention and continued support. In some cases the attention was extraordinarily close, and for this I am particularly thankful.

I also want to express my appreciation to Marlies Van Hoof and Marie-Ange Catotti, secretaries to the Department of Political and Social Sciences at the European University Institute, for their skillful typing and other help in preparing the manuscript for publication.

*Evidence, Argument, and Persuasion
in the Policy Process*

ONE

Policy Analysis and Public Deliberation

As politicians know only too well but social scientists too often forget, public policy is made of language. Whether in written or oral form, argument is central in all stages of the policy process. Discussion goes on in any organization, private or public, and in any political system, even a dictatorship; but it is so much at the heart of democratic politics and policy that democracy has been called a system of government by discussion. Political parties, the electorate, the legislature, the executive, the courts, the media, interest groups, and independent experts all engage in a continuous process of debate and reciprocal persuasion.

This process, as liberal theorists from John Stuart Mill and Walter Bagehot to Lord Lindsay and Ernest Barker have described it, begins with expressions of general concerns and ends in concrete decisions. Each stage of deliberation has its own function and its own organ. Parties identify issues and formulate programs; the electorate discusses issues and candidates and expresses a majority in favor of one of the programs; the legislative majority translates programs into laws, in constant debate with the opposition; finally, the discussion is carried forward to the chief executive and the cabinet, where it is translated into specific policies. Each of the stages and organs of public delib-

deliberate

eration is independent, but only within the limits, and as a part, of the entire process: "the free and sovereign thing is the whole process of discussion."[1]

This is an idealized model of democratic policy-making. It overlooks the play of power and influence, the uneven distribution of knowledge, the low level of active citizen participation, and many other factors that figure prominently in modern theories of public policy. But it emphasizes something that these theories have neglected—the extraordinary potential of persuasion and the centrality of two-way discussion to democracy.[2]

Every politician understands that arguments are needed not only to clarify his position with respect to an issue, but to bring other people around to this position. Even when a policy is best explained by the actions of groups seeking selfish goals, those who seek to justify the policy must appeal to the public interest and the intellectual merits of the case.[3] Perhaps these are only rationalizations, but even rationalizations are important since they become integral parts of political discourse. We miss a great deal if we try to understand policy-making solely in terms of power, influence, and bargaining, to the exclusion of debate and argument.

Argumentation is the key process through which citizens and policymakers arrive at moral judgments and policy choices. Public discussion mobilizes the knowledge, experience, and interest of many people, while focusing their attention on a limited range of issues. Each participant is encouraged to adjust his view of reality, and even to change his values, as a result of the process of reciprocal persuasion. In this way, discussion can produce results that are beyond the capabilities of authoritarian or technocratic methods of policy-making.

1. Ernest Barker, *Reflections on Government* (New York: Oxford University Press, 1958), 37.

2. Charles E. Lindblom, *Politics and Markets* (New York: Basic Books, 1977).

3. John W. Kingdon, *Agendas, Alternatives, and Public Policies* (Boston: Little, Brown, 1984), 131–34.

THE INSTITUTIONALIZATION OF DISCUSSION

However, this extraordinary potential can be realized only with the help of appropriate rules and procedures. Unregulated discussion easily ends in unending dispute and even in violence. An unorganized deliberative body is open to various forms of disruption, such as filibustering.

To avoid or reduce these dangers, public deliberation has been carefully institutionalized in all modern democracies. Today's elaborate codes of parliamentary, electoral, administrative, and judicial procedure are the fruit of centuries of experience in coping with practical problems of public deliberation. The general purpose of these procedures is to insure the hearing of many opinions without compromising the need to reach a conclusion. Their importance is such that the history of democratic government is, in a real sense, the history of various procedures devised to institutionalize and regulate public deliberation.

While rules of debate have hardened into institutions in the traditional forums of public deliberation, in newer arenas of debate such as nuclear safety, technology assessment, and environmental and health regulation appropriate procedures and standards of argument are still lacking. One reason it has proved difficult to institutionalize debate in these and other areas of policy-making is that the issues under discussion here are seldom purely technical or purely political. Rather, they often are of a type that Alvin Weinberg has called "trans-scientific"—questions of fact that can be stated in the language of science but are, in principle or in practice, unanswerable by science.[4]

A typical example is the determination of the health effects of low-level radiation. It has been calculated that in order to determine by direct experimentation, at the 95 percent confidence level, whether a dosage of X-ray radiation of 150 millirems would increase the spontaneous mutation in mice by ½ percent would require about eight billion mice. Time and resource con-

4. Alvin Weinberg, "Science and Trans-Science," *Minerva* 10, no. 2 (April 1972): 209–22.

straints make such an experiment practically impossible. Similarly, the choice of a dose-response function to determine the "virtually safe" dose of a toxic substance must be treated at present as a trans-scientific question. There are literally thousands of mathematical functions that fit the experimental data equally well, but no firm scientific basis now exists for choosing among the different possibilities. However, the choice of a particular function has a major effect on regulatory decisions.

When science, technology, and public policy intersect, different attitudes, perspectives, and rules of argument come into sharp conflict. Scientific criteria of truth clash with legal standards of evidence and with political notions of what constitutes sufficient ground for action. Factual conclusions are not easily separable from considerations having to do with the plausibility of the opponent's assumptions and his selection of the evidence or choice of methodology. And because there seems to be no objective way of checking the conclusions of analysis, the credibility of the expert becomes as important as his competence.

Increasingly, public debates about regulatory decisions, nuclear safety, technology assessment, and similar trans-scientific issues tend to resemble adversary proceedings in a court of law, but with an important difference—the lack of generally accepted rules of procedure. Some participants are able to take advantage of the relative informality of the process, but to scientists even codified adversary procedures seem inappropriate and alien to their tradition. In science the issue is not a witness's credibility but his specific competence—his ability to establish scientific truth—and this is not reliably established by an adversary debate. Hence various proposals to resolve disputes about scientific issues with policy implications by carefully breaking down a problem into purely technical and purely political components. Experts should deal only with the technical issues, turning their evaluations over to the political process for determination of the appropriate policy response.

For example, the "science court" proposed by Arthur Kantrowitz would only examine, and decide upon, questions of scientific fact. After the evidence has been presented, questioned, and defended, the panel of judges (who are established experts in areas adjacent to the dispute) issue a report in which the points of agreement among the experts are given. The report may also suggest specific research projects to clarify points that remain unsettled.[5]

But how can one separate the scientific from the political and value components of policy issues that encompass both? And if trans-scientific questions do not come within the purview of the scientific court, why use a quasi-judicial procedure? If the question is unambiguously scientific, then the procedures of science rather than quasi-legal ones are appropriate. Where the issues cannot be settled with existing scientific knowledge or from research that could be carried out reasonably rapidly and without excessive expense, then the answers must be trans-scientific and an adversary procedure that involves both experts and generalists seems the best alternative.[6]

Dialectical confrontation between generalists and experts often succeeds in bringing out unstated assumptions, conflicting interpretations of the facts, and the risks posed by new projects. Technical experts are naturally biased in the assessment of their proposals and are more likely to be skeptical of any evidence of possible adverse effects than someone less committed to that particular project. The initial assumption is that the innovation will achieve what the innovator claims for it and that it will have no negative consequences that could reduce the attractiveness of its practical implementation. For example, the consciousness of the dangers inherent in nuclear engineering in the United States and Western Europe is largely the result of public debate. Where nuclear technology has been allowed to develop according to its own logic, unhampered by criticism and public concern, as in the Soviet Union, it has produced few of the safety features (such as containment shells for pressurized water reactors) that are now standard in the West.

Thus, technological expertise cannot be relied upon to discover the characteristic risks and the social implications of new

5. Arthur Kantrowitz, "Proposal for an Institution for Scientific Judgment," *Science* 156, no. 3,776 (12 May 1967): 763–64.
6. Weinberg, "Science and Trans-Science," 214–16.

technologies. The essential need today is an improvement in the methods and conditions of critical debate and their institutionalization at all levels of policy-making. Actually, attempts to develop methods of critical inquiry adapted to the process of public deliberation go back to the origins of democracy.

Building on the practice of government by discussion in the city-state, the Greeks developed a general technique of critical discourse which they called dialectic. This is a method of argumentation characterized not so much by the form of reasoning (though discussion by question and answer came to be regarded as its paradigmatic form) as by the nature of its premises and the social context of its applications. Logic and mathematics start from axioms, or propositions deduced from axioms, while the premises of dialectic are merely plausible. The starting point of a dialectic argument is not abstract assumptions but points of view already present in the community; its conclusion is not a formal proof, but a shared understanding of the issue under discussion; and while scientific disciplines are specialized forms of knowledge, available only to the experts, dialectic can be used by everyone since, as Aristotle put it, we all have occasion to criticize or defend an argument.

For the Greeks dialectic had three main uses. First, as a method of critical inquiry into the foundations and assumptions of the various specialized disciplines. Second, as a technique for arguing in favor of one's own opinions and a procedure for clarifying controversial issues. Finally, as an educational process that transforms the common man into an informed citizen and the specialist into a person able to communicate with his fellow citizens.

This ancient notion of dialectic is quite relevant to our inquiry into the role of analysis in public deliberation. In fact, it seems to capture the essential elements of that role much better than the stereotyped characterization of policy analysis found in current textbooks. Like dialectic, policy analysis usually starts with plausible premises, with contestable and shifting viewpoints, not with indisputable principles or hard facts. Like dialectic, it does not produce formal proofs but only persuasive arguments. The key problem facing both dialecticians and analysts is how to base plausible inferences on values or opinions when hard facts are not available. Finally, policy analysis, like dialectic, contributes to public deliberation through criticism, advocacy, and education. Good policy analysis is more than data analysis or a modeling exercise; it also provides standards of argument and an intellectual structure for public discourse. Even when its conclusions are not accepted, its categories and language, its criticism of traditional approaches, and its advocacy of new ideas affect—even condition—the policy debate.

THE ARGUMENTATIVE FUNCTION OF POLICY ANALYSIS

The purpose of this book is to discover the main implications of a dialectic conception of policy analysis. In it I attempt to develop a single idea: the notion that in a system of government by discussion, analysis—even professional analysis—has less to do with formal techniques of problem solving than with the process of argument.

The job of analysts consists in large part of producing evidence and arguments to be used in the course of public debate. Its crucial argumentative aspect is what distinguishes policy analysis from the academic social sciences on the one hand, and from problem-solving methodologies such as operations research on the other. The arguments analysts produce may be more or less technical, more or less sophisticated, but they must persuade if they are to be taken seriously in the forums of public deliberation. Thus, analysts, like lawyers, politicians, and others who make a functional use of language, will always be involved in all the technical problems of language, including rhetorical problems.[7]

Rhetoric is the craft of persuasion, the study of all the ways of doing things with words. The Athenians used to make annual sacrifices to the goddess of persuasion (Peitho) in recognition of the extraordinary power of language. Today persuasion is often

7. Northrop Frye, *Anatomy of Criticism* (Princeton, N.J.: Princeton University Press, 1957), 331.

regarded as a dishonest or merely "rationalizing" use of arguments; it is propaganda, brainwashing, manipulation of public opinion. Persuasion can indeed be used in these ways. But in free debate, persuasion is a two-way interchange, a method of mutual learning through discourse. Real debate not only lets the participants promote their own views and interests, but also encourages them to adjust their views of reality and even to change their values as a result of the process.

A persuasive argument is not a logical demonstration, but it does not become irrational or mere rationalization because of this. Most value judgments are formed in persuasive interchange. To reduce reason to logical calculation and proof about whatever does not matter enough to engage commitment is, as Wayne C. Booth has written, to create a torn picture of the world, with all our values on one side and all our rational faculties on the other.[8] Since to say anything of importance in public policy requires value judgments, this artificial separation between values and rational capacities is a threat to all notions of public deliberation and defensible policy choices.

As I will show in the next chapter, even technical policy analysts cannot dispense with persuasion. On the one hand, facts and values are so intertwined in policy-making that factual arguments unaided by persuasion seldom play a significant role in public debate. On the other hand, persuasion is needed in order to increase both the acceptability of advice and the willingness to act on less than conclusive evidence. To explain and defend a reasonable course of action under circumstances where the theoretical optimum is either unknown or practically unattainable is an essential part of the analyst's job.

Feasibility analysis, to be discussed in chapter 4, is perhaps the best illustration of the necessary interplay of empirical and persuasive arguments. Fashioning mutual understandings about the boundaries of the possible in public policy is arguably the most important contribution that analysts can make to public debate. However, calculating optimal or second-best solutions

8. *Modern Dogma and the Rhetoric of Assent* (Chicago: University of Chicago Press, 1974), 116.

within given constraints is only the static part of feasibility analysis; the dynamic and more important part is discovering means to push out the boundaries of the possible. Doing this requires both objective analysis and persuasion: what is possible often depends on what the political system considers fair or acceptable. Many policy constraints can be eased only by changing attitudes and values; as already noted, this always involves a certain amount of persuasion.

ARGUMENTATION AND EVALUATION

Persuasive arguments play an even larger role in evaluative discourse. Whenever new evaluative criteria or a reform of old criteria are being considered, it is open to anyone to put forward a proposal as to what the criteria should be and to use persuasion in order to influence others to accept the proposal.

The characteristic difficulty of policy evaluation is precisely the multiplicity of admissible standards. Citizens, legislators, administrators, judges, experts, the media—all contribute their particular perspectives and criteria. This variety of viewpoints is not only unavoidable in a pluralistic society; it is also necessary to the vitality of a system of government by discussion. Nevertheless, as Northrop Frye has remarked in the context of literary criticism, there seems to be no reason why the larger understanding of public policy to which these separate perspectives are contributing should remain forever invisible to the different evaluators, as the coral atoll is to the polyp.

Multiple policy evaluation should also be possible. It would recognize the legitimacy of the different perspectives but would also seek—by making these perspectives more aware of one another—to reach a level of understanding and appreciation that is more than the sum of the separate evaluations. The purpose is not to construct a grand model that would combine all the partial perspectives into one general criterion of good policy— a weighted average, as it were, of equity, effectiveness, legality, and any other relevant standard—but to contribute to a shared understanding of the multiple perspectives involved.

Evaluation will be discussed in detail in chapter 8. Here I will mention only one aspect of the subject—the evaluation of analysis and other types of research with policy implications. The assessment of policy arguments, like the assessment of scientific or legal arguments, necessarily involves formalities. When the issues under discussion require complex patterns of reasoning and large amounts of data of doubtful reliability and relevance, explicit rules of evidence become particularly important. A good example is the judicial law of evidence with its sophisticated distinctions among proofs of facts, testimony, hearsay, presumptions, interpretations, and other sources of information.

In chapter 3 I introduce a number of distinctions (for example, among data, information, and evidence) whose main purpose is to facilitate the evaluation of policy arguments. The importance of drawing distinctions that are usually overlooked in conventional treatments of policy analysis can be illustrated with reference to the categories "evidence" and "argument." The argument is the link that connects data and information with the conclusions of an analytic study. The structure of the argument will typically be a complex blend of factual statements and subjective evaluations. Along with mathematical and logical deductions it will include statistical, empirical, and analogical inferences, references to expert opinion, estimates of benefits and costs, and caveats and provisos of different kinds. This unavoidable complexity makes any direct, informal testing of the argument quite impossible. Whatever testing is done must rely on a variety of standards that depend on the analytic methods employed, on the plausibility and robustness of the conclusions, and on agreed-upon criteria of adequacy and effectiveness.

The nature of the evidence is crucial in this kind of testing, since an incorrect assessment of its strength and suitability before it is included in the argument can lead to pitfalls in drawing conclusions. Evidence is not synonymous with data or information. It is information selected from the available stock and introduced at a specific point in the argument in order to persuade a particular audience of the truth or falsity of a statement. Selecting inappropriate data or models, placing them at a wrong point in the argument, or choosing a style of presentation that is not suitable for the intended audience, can destróy the effectiveness of information used as evidence, regardless of its intrinsic cognitive value. Thus, criteria for assessing evidence are different from those used for assessing facts. Facts can be evaluated in terms of more or less objective canons, but evidence must be evaluated in accordance with a number of factors peculiar to a given situation, such as the specific nature of the case, the type of audience, the prevailing rules of evidence, or the credibility of the analyst.

Disciplines like history and law, which depend on information that cannot automatically be assumed to be reliable or relevant, explicitly recognize evidence as an autonomous conceptual category. Policy analysis, too, often involves large amounts of data of doubtful reliability and relevance, but problems of evidence have not received the same attention here.

For instance, according to a view that is widespread among analysts, a good policy model should resemble as much as possible the formalized models of the more successful "hard" sciences. Accordingly, there is a dangerous tendency to regard model outputs as facts, rather than as evidence to be used in an argument together with other data and information. As a result, "the documentation of models and source data is in an unbelievably primitive state.... Poor documentation makes it next to impossible for anyone but the modeler to reproduce the modeling results and probe the effects of changes to the model. Sometimes a model is kept proprietary by its builder for commercial reasons. The customer is allowed to see only the results, not the assumptions."[9]

Such gross disregard for the most elementary rules of evidence is a direct consequence of the failure to recognize the crucial argumentative aspect of policy analysis. In turn, this failure can be explained by the adherence of most analysts to a methodology that is more concerned with what decisions are made than with how they are made, or how they may be justified in the forums of public deliberation.

9. Martin Greenberger, Matthew A. Crenson, and Brian L. Crissey, *Models in the Policy Process* (New York: Russell Sage Foundation, 1976), 338.

DECISIONISM

The image that lies behind this methodology has been called decisionism—the "vision of a limited number of political actors engaged in making calculated choices among clearly conceived alternatives."[10] An actor's choices are considered rational if they can be explained as the choosing of the best means to achieve given objectives. In this view the economic model of choice becomes the appropriate paradigm for all policy problems.

For example, a well-known textbook on policy analysis introduces its subject matter as follows: "How choices should be made—the whole problem of allocating scarce resources among competing ends—is the stuff of economics and the subject of this book."[11] Similar statements can be found in the writings of influential authors like Hitch, McKean, Enthoven, and Quade.[12]

In order to decide rationally the policymaker must specify his objectives; lay out the alternatives by which the objectives may be accomplished; evaluate the consequences of each alternative; and choose the action that maximizes net benefits. If the recipe sounds familiar it is because the logical structure of allocative decisions is the same whether the decisions are taken by individual consumers, by private entrepreneurs, or by public managers and policymakers. Hence the appeal to a generalized logic of choice which decisionists found ready-made in microeconomics and decision theory. Moreover, since the logic of choice has been investigated primarily in the context of market transactions, some writers have argued that the main, if not the only, object of policy analysis is to extend the principles of rational

10. Judith Shklar, "Decisionism," in C. J. Friedrich, ed., *Nomos*, vol. 7, *Rational Decision* (New York: Atherton, 1964), 3–17.

11. Edith Stokey and Richard Zeckhauser, *A Primer for Policy Analysis* (New York: W. W. Norton, 1978), 22.

12. Charles J. Hitch and Roland McKean, *The Economics of Defense in the Nuclear Age* (Cambridge: Harvard University Press, 1962); Alain C. Enthoven and K. Wayne Smith, *How Much is Enough?* (New York: Harper and Row, 1971); E. S. Quade, *Analysis for Public Decisions*, 2d ed. (Amsterdam: North-Holland, 1982).

choice from the sphere of private economic transactions to that of public policy-making. In fact, rational policy-making, decision making, problem solving, and policy analysis become nearly synonymous terms. For example, the recipe for maximizing net benefits may be interpreted either as a description of ideal policy-making or as a prescription for policy analysis. The underlying notion of rationality is the same in both cases: rationality is maximizing something, choosing the best means to a given end.

The view of policy analysis as decision theory "writ large" has considerable intuitive appeal and provides a useful way of formulating a variety of practical problems: whether to use a particular vaccine to halt the spread of a threatened epidemic; where to build a dam; how to reduce the response time of the fire department of a big city. Not surprisingly, these or similar examples are the standard illustrations used in conventional textbooks.

The decisionist approach was developed during the Second World War and was given emphasis and formal statement in the early 1950s at the Rand Corporation and other policy-oriented think tanks. It is a conceptual compound that includes elements from operations research and management science, from microeconomics and decision theory, and a dash of social and behavioral science. A continuous line of development runs from the wartime studies of military operations, of logistics and tactics, to the early industrial applications of new quantitative methods, to systems analysis, and then to policy analysis. Technical efficiency as a goal or criterion of choice has been replaced by economic efficiency, which in turn has been tempered by considerations of equity and political feasibility. But the original analytic framework is still clearly recognizable.

The early practitioners of this approach claimed to be able to give useful advice by applying scientific methods of analysis to data collected from actual operations. In fact the situations investigated by operations researchers during the war fit the natural science paradigm rather well. Military operations could be regarded as representative of a class of repetitive situations where models built up in response to earlier examples of the situation could be checked against later examples, monitored while proposals for improved actions were in use, and used to detect their own dwindling validity as the situation changed.[13]

An important characteristic of early studies of military and industrial operations was a reasonable clarity in the definition of the role of analysts and decision makers. Whether the users of analysis were high-level military officers or high-level managers, analysis was done primarily or even (because of the requirement of military or industrial secrecy) exclusively for them. The analyst did not have to address any audience other than the decision maker, or a small group of decision makers, who had commissioned the study. Problems of communication and implementation could be safely assumed to be the responsibility of a well-defined hierarchical authority, and the same authority would ensure legitimacy and provide criteria of quality and effectiveness.

By the 1960s, however, the nature of the problems analysts were investigating, and the organizational and political context in which they operated, had radically changed. The problems claiming analytic attention were becoming broader and more complex. Strategic, rather than tactical, issues loomed increasingly important, while subjective uncertainty was seen to be more crucial then the statistical regularities assumed in earlier models. At the same time, the growing role of analysis in public debates meant that analysts—no longer discreet advisors to the prince but actors in a political process in which advocacy and persuasion could not be neatly separated from objective analysis—had to pay attention to questions of equity and political feasibility.

In the early 1970s *policy analysis* came to replace *systems analysis* as the professional label denoting the activity of analysts who were concerned with public issues. This terminological change was meant to suggest a synthesis of the conflicting logics of economic and political rationality. In practice, since political science seemed unable to provide a set of concepts and analytic techniques comparable to the strong normative structure of micro-

13. Hylton Boothroyd, *Articulate Intervention* (London: Taylor and Francis, 1978), 113.

economics, the majority of policy analysts remained firmly committed to a decisionist methodology.

THE LIMITATIONS OF DECISIONISM

The limitations and biases of the decisionist approach are perhaps less obvious than its merits, but they affect almost every aspect of the teaching and practice of policy analysis. However, I shall restrict my critical remarks to a few points of particular relevance for my subsequent discussion. The purpose is to illustrate the kinds of issues and arguments that this approach tends to exclude from analysis.

To begin with, the decisionist approach assumes a unitary decision maker, or a group acting as a unit, and is not immediately applicable to situations involving two or more actors with different objectives. The model of rational choice that underlies this approach has been developed for an individual who wishes to be consistent and expresses this consistency in the way he orders his preferences and evaluates the probabilities of uncertain events. When several individuals are involved, the model does not require them to agree on their orderings and evaluations; each may be rational (that is, consistent) in holding quite divergent views. If a joint decision is required, they will have to resolve their differences through interactive processes like negotiation and persuasion, about which the model is silent.

A fortiori, this methodology ignores conflicts between the interests and perceptions of different government agencies. But whenever such conflicts are present, important questions arise about the appropriate assumptions regarding the behavior of other public agencies in the formulation of policy by any particular agency. As I argue in chapter 6, all policy instruments are effectively constrained within certain ranges by political and administrative considerations. Therefore, it is important for policymakers to know which variables are in fact within their control and to what extent, and in this respect a unitary model of policymaking is not very useful.

Another key assumption is that there is no essential distinction between policies and decisions, so that all policy problems can be discussed in the language of decision making. But as Philip Selznick has pointed out,

> decisionmaking is one of those fashionable phrases that may well obscure more than it illuminates. It has an air of significance, of reference to important events; and the mere use of the phrase seems to suggest that something definite has been scientifically isolated. But decisions are with us always, at every level of experience, in every organism. The general features of all choice, or of all social choice, may some day be convincingly stated. But it will still be necessary to distinguish the more and the less trivial; and, if there is any order in this phenomenon, to identify some kinds of decisions, linking them to the distinctive problems or situations out of which they arise.[14]

In fact, contrary to a widespread belief, decision theory does not apply to decision making in general, but only to choice situations of a rather special type. The decision of decision theory is a choice that _must_ be made in the situation immediately confronting the decision maker, taking into consideration the probable consequences of each possible course of action in the _present_ situation. Future benefits, for example, must be defined in terms of the way they are assessed today, even though there is no reason to assume that this will coincide with the assessment of those benefits in the future.[15]

Confronted with two alternatives, the decision maker of decision theory chooses _as if_ the benefits from one were greater than (or at least equal to) the benefits from the other in the present situation. As John Tukey points out, this choice does not assert anything about the actual state of affairs, or about the consequences in other situations of acting as if the chosen alternative were the best of the available ones. Decisions to act in this way are attempts to do as well as possible in specific situations,

14. _Leadership in Administration_ (New York: Harper and Row, 1964), 56.
15. Amartya K. Sen, "Rational Fools: A Critique of the Behavioral Foundations of Economic Theory," _Philosophy and Public Affairs_ 6, no. 4 (Summer 1977): 317–44.

to choose wisely among the available gambles.[16] Decision theorists are fond of quoting Blaise Pascal's "il faut parier, il faut
choisir" (one has to bet, one has to choose), and problems connected with games of chance have supplied the original paradigm for probability theory and its modern offspring, decision
theory.

There are situations, in private life as well as in business and
in government, where individuals do in fact choose under the
conditions covered by the theory. But in many other situations
the theory is not particularly useful, either prescriptively or
descriptively.

Thus, important policy decisions are more than attempts to
do as well as possible in the situation immediately confronting
the policymaker. They are taken after careful deliberation and
are judged by their long-run effects rather than by their immediate consequences. Once taken, they are retained for some
time, providing direction and consistency to the various activities
of government. As a former presidential adviser puts it, "Most
presidential decisions are too far-reaching and too irrevocable
to be taken in haste, when the facts are uncertain, when the
choices are unclear, or when the long-range consequences are
not as discernible as the immediate reactions and results."[17] What
Theodore Sorensen describes here are not decisions in the sense
of decision theory, but policy judgments that are more usefully
discussed in the language of prudential discourse.

A third limitation of decisionism is its exclusive preoccupation
with outcomes and lack of concern for the processes whereby
the outcomes are produced. A lack of concern for process is
justified in some situations. If the correctness or fairness of the
outcome can be determined unambiguously, the manner in
which the decision is made is often immaterial; only results count.
But when the factual or value premises are moot, when there
are no generally accepted criteria of rightness, the procedure of

---

16. John W. Tukey, "Conclusions Versus Decisions," *Technometrics* 2, no. 4
(Nov. 1960): 423–33.

17. Theodore C. Sorensen, *Decision-Making in the White House* (New York:
Columbia University Press, 1963), 30.

decision-making acquires special significance and cannot be treated as purely instrumental.

Even in formal decision analysis the explicit recognition of uncertainty forces a significant departure from a strict orientation toward outcomes. Under conditions of uncertainty different alternatives correspond to different probability distributions of the consequences, so that it is no longer possible to determine unambiguously what the optimal decision is. Hence, the usual criterion of rationality—according to which an action is rational if it can be explained as the choosing of the best means to achieve given objectives—is replaced by the weaker notion of consistency. The rational decision maker is no longer an optimizer, strictly speaking. All that is required now, and all that the principle of maximizing expected utility guarantees, is that the choice be consistent with the decision maker's valuations of the probability and utility of the various consequences.[18] Notice that consistency is a procedural, not a substantive, criterion.

Exclusive preoccupation with outcomes is a serious limitation of decisionism, since social processes seldom have only instrumental value for the people who engage in them. In most areas of social activity, "the processes and rules that constitute the enterprise and define the roles of its participants matter quite apart from any identifiable "end state" that is ultimately produced. Indeed in many cases it is the process itself that matters *most to those* who take part in it."[19]

Thus, as John Dewey once observed, the most important thing about popular voting and majority rule is less the actual outcome of the voter choice than the fact that the electoral process compels prior recourse to methods of discussion, consultation, and persuasion, and the resulting modification of views to accommodate the opinion of the minority.[20]

Again, knowledge of the outcomes, even when they can be measured precisely, is not the type of information that citizens

18. Dennis W. Lindley, *Making Decisions* (New York: Wiley-Interscience, 1971), 6.
19. Laurence H. Tribe, "Policy Science: Analysis or Ideology?", *Philosophy and Public Affairs* 2, no. 1 (Fall 1972): 83.
20. *The Public and Its Problems* (New York: Holt, 1927), 207–09.

and policymakers find most useful in many situations. Simply knowing that outcomes are good or bad, without knowing the process that has produced them, does not tell decision makers and critics very much about what to do. As I will show in chapter 8, knowledge of process is often essential for purposes of evaluation and learning since it provides information that outcome measures are almost sure to miss.

The usefulness of the decisionist approach to public policy-making is further limited by the fact that in politics, as in the law (but not the market), decisions must always be justified. Justificatory arguments play an important role in the policy debate but are alien to the philosophy of decisionism. In part this is because the reasons given to justify or explain a decision are often different from the decision maker's original motives or "revealed preferences" and thus appear to be mere rationalizations. But as I will show in greater detail in chapter 2, it is not necessarily dishonest or merely "rationalizing" to use arguments based on considerations different from those that led to the adoption of a certain position. There is no unique way to construct an argument: data and evidence can be selected in a wide variety of ways from available information, and there are several alternative methods for analysis and ways of ordering values. There is nothing intrinsically reprehensible in selecting the particular combination of data, facts, values, and analytic methods that seems to be most appropriate to convince the people who have to accept or carry out the decision. If analysts are reluctant or unable to provide such postdecision justifications or explanations, policymakers have no choice but to turn elsewhere for assistance.

Because decisionism is an internally consistent doctrine, the various limitations noted above—the assumption of the unitary decision maker, the lack of concern for process, the failure to distinguish among different classes of decisions and to recognize the role of argument and persuasion in decision making—are all intimately related. Their cumulative effect is to produce an overintellectualized version of policy analysis which gives undue emphasis to the more technical aspects of a subject that in fact should be concerned with the whole of the policy process.

Decisionists look upon policy problems as if they were puzzles for which, given clear goals and sufficient information, correct solutions always exist and can be found by calculation rather than by the exercise of political skills. Hence, policy-making can be intelligent or rational only if it is preceded by systematic analysis of the alternatives in all their implications. To act rationally is, according to this view, always to do two things: to work out a plan of action and to put into practice what the plan prescribes. It is, in Gilbert Ryle's phrase, to do a bit of theory and then to do a bit of practice.[21]

But it is notoriously possible to plan well and to implement the plan stupidly. Moreover, by the original assumption, in order to be rational the planning process itself would have to be preceded by yet another process of planning to plan. This infinite regress reduces to absurdity the notion that for a decision or policy to be intelligent it must be guided by a prior intellectual operation. "Intelligent" cannot be defined in terms of "intellectual" or "knowing how" in terms of "knowing that."[22]

Someone without a knowledge of medicine can hardly be a good surgeon, but excellence at surgery is not the same thing as knowledge of medical science, nor is it a direct result of it. Like surgery, the making of policy and the giving of policy advice are exercises of skills, and we do not judge skillful performance by the amount of information stored in the head of the performer or by the amount of formal planning. Rather, we judge it by criteria like good timing and attention to details; by the capacity to recognize the limits of the possible, to use limitations creatively, and to learn from one's mistakes; by the ability not only to show what should be done, but to persuade people to do what they know should be done.

Perhaps the most serious limitation of the decisionist view is not that it is wrong per se, but that it has led to a serious imbalance in the way we think about policy-making. The following chapters will attempt to provide a more realistic view of the uses of knowledge and analysis in policy deliberation and a better appreciation of the skills needed to transform ideas into actions.

21. *The Concept of Mind* (New York: Barnes and Noble, 1949), 29.
22. Ibid., 32.

T W O

Analysis as Argument

Policy analysts of the decisionist persuasion would like to project
the image of technical, nonpartisan problem solvers who map
out the alternatives open to the policymaker and evaluate their
consequences by means of mathematical models or other objective techniques of analysis. The analyst's job is only to determine the best means to achieve given goals. He must be neutral
about ends, since discussion of goals and values is necessarily
subjective and unscientific. Analysis that aspires to be objective and scientific can deal only with factual statements. Hence,
a sharp distinction should be drawn between professional policy
analysis, and policy advocacy or policy deliberation. Professional policy analysis begins only after the relevant values have
been stipulated, either by an authoritative policymaker or
through the aggregation of citizen preferences in the political
process.

This image of the analyst's art is grossly misleading. I would
like to suggest a more accurate one. The policy analyst is a producer of policy arguments, more similar to a lawyer—a specialist
in legal arguments—than to an engineer or a scientist. His basic
skills are not algorithmical but argumentative: the ability to
probe assumptions critically, to produce and evaluate evi-

dence, to keep many threads in hand, to draw for an argument from many disparate sources, to communicate effectively. He recognizes that to say anything of importance in public policy requires value judgments, which must be explained and justified, and is willing to apply his skills to any topic relevant to public discussion.

The image of the analyst as problem solver is misleading because the conclusions of policy analysis seldom can be rigorously proved. Demonstrative proof that a particular alternative ought to be chosen in a particular situation is possible only if the context of the policy problem is artificially restricted. One must assume that there is no disagreement about the appropriate formulation of the problem, no conflict of values and interests, and that the solution is, somehow, self-executing. Also, the analyst should have all the relevant information, including full knowledge of present and future preferences and of all consequences of all possible alternatives.

The impossibility of proving what the correct action is in most practical situations weakens the credibility of analysis as problem solving, but it does not imply that information, discussion, and argument are irrelevant. We reason even when we do not calculate—in setting norms and formulating problems, in presenting evidence for or against a proposal, in offering or rejecting criticism. In all these cases we do not demonstrate, but argue.

Argumentation differs from formal demonstration in three important respects. First, demonstration is possible only within a formalized system of axioms and rules of inference. Argumentation does not start from axioms but from opinions, values, or contestable viewpoints; it makes use of logical inferences but is not exhausted in deductive systems of formal statements. Second, a demonstration is designed to convince anybody who has the requisite technical knowledge, while argumentation is always directed to a particular audience and attempts to elicit or increase the adherence of the members of the audience to the theses that are presented for their consent. Finally, argumentation does not aim at gaining purely intellectual agreement but at inciting action, or at least at creating a disposition to act at the appropriate moment.[1]

It will be noticed that the distinctive features of argumentation are precisely those which characterize dialectic and rhetorical reasoning. Thus, to recognize that policy analysis has less to do with proof and computation than with the process of argument is to make contact with an old philosophical tradition that defines rationality not in instrumental terms, but as the ability to provide acceptable reasons for one's choices and actions. By restricting the role of reason to discovering appropriate means to given ends, instrumental rationality relegates values, criteria, judgments, and opinions to the domain of the irrational or the purely subjective. Analysis-as-argument holds that this narrowing of discourse goes against the grain of a system of government by discussion. In order to influence public deliberation in significant ways, analysts must open themselves to a wider range of argument than is allowed by the methodology of decisionism.

It is true that practicing policy analysts often engage in argumentative discourse: they debate values, question objectives, agree or disagree about assumptions, and advocate or justify courses of action on the basis of less-than-conclusive evidence. What is problematic about these practices is not their content but the fact that they remain unexamined and that in consequence crucial aspects of analysis escape critical evaluation. In this chapter I discuss some of the most significant rhetorical uses of policy analysis.

NORM SETTING

It is widely assumed that public deliberation and public policy are primarily concerned with setting goals and finding the means to achieve them. Actually, the most important function both of public deliberation and of policy-making is defining the norms

1. Chaim Perelman, *The Realm of Rhetoric* (Notre Dame: University of Notre Dame Press, 1982), 4–7.

that determine when certain conditions are to be regarded as policy problems. Objective conditions are seldom so compelling and so unambiguous that they set the policy agenda or dictate the appropriate conceptualization. In the 1950s the issue of poverty was a minor one in American public consciousness. In the 1960s, with little change in the distribution of income, it became a significant part of public policies.[2]

What had changed were attitudes and views on poverty, and beliefs in the capacity of government to find solutions to social problems. A particularly important new element was the emergence of an intellectual consensus about the "structural" causes of poverty. As Charles Murray writes, "The emergence of the structural view of the poverty problem was unexpected and rapid. At the beginning of 1962, no one was talking about poverty; by the end of 1963 it was the hottest domestic policy topic other than civil rights. But it was not just 'poverty' that was being talked about. 'Structural poverty' was now the issue."[3]

As was pointed out above, in the decisionist view rational policy analysis can begin only after the relevant values have been authoritatively determined. In fact, these values are neither given nor constant, but are themselves a function of the policy-making process that they are supposed to guide. Of the problems with which a democratic government is expected to be concerned today, many were not regarded as policy problems a century or even a few decades ago. Of those that were so regarded (such as the relief of extreme poverty), the norms have radically changed. Yet the process that has brought about these changes in norms is the same historical process which these norms have guided.[4]

Far from waiting passively for the stipulation of public values to be served, policy analysts and researchers are often deeply involved in the process of norm setting. President Lyndon John-

2. Joseph R. Gusfield, *Drinking-Driving and the Symbolic Order* (Chicago: University of Chicago Press, 1981), 4.

3. *Losing Ground* (New York: Basic Books, 1984), 27.

4. Geoffrey Vickers, *The Art of Judgment* (London: Chapman and Hall, 1965), 120–35.

son's "war" on poverty is one example.[5] Another example is the policy innovation represented by pollution-control laws with clear goals and timetables to achieve them, such as the 1970 Clean Air Act and the 1972 Federal Water Pollution Control Act. This legislation was significantly influenced by a theory of "agency capture," according to which vague statutory language was a cause of the capture of regulatory agencies by business. The proposed remedy was statutes that have clear goals, set fixed deadlines for achieving them, and empower citizen groups to take slow-moving agencies to court.

These ideas were incorporated in a number of influential textbooks and were eventually adopted by Congress in the popularized version provided by members of the Ralph Nader organization and other policy advocates.[6] The final result of the combined efforts of researchers and activists was a radical resetting of norms relating to environmental and health protection. Judged by the new norms the traditional regulatory structure—based on informal negotiation with industry, weak enforcement by state agencies, and a large measure of administrative discretion—suddenly appeared inadequate and prone to corruption. A major shift from decentralized regulation and voluntary compliance toward regulation at the national level by means of legally enforceable standards was the legislative response to the new norms.

Conceptually, norm setting can be distinguished from norm using—the search for solutions that satisfy current norms. This distinction is analogous to the traditional dichotomy of policy and administration. The policy/administration dichotomy has been used to support the doctrine that political leaders make policy while the task of administrators and experts is to find the appropriate means to implement it. But it is not the case that policy settles everything down to a certain point while administration deals with everything below that point. Policy and

5. Henry J. Aaron, *Politics and the Professor* (Washington, D.C.: Brookings Institution, 1978), chap. 2.

6. Alfred Marcus, "The Environmental Protection Agency," in James Q. Wilson, ed., *The Politics of Regulation* (New York: Basic Books, 1980), 267–303.

administration do not occupy two separate spheres of action, but interact throughout the entire process of policy-making.

One reason why it is difficult in practice to separate policy from administration, or norm setting from norm using, is that legislative mandates are often so vague, ambiguous, or contradictory that there are no clear standards for administrators and experts to apply. Even when the statutes attempt to define goals with great precision, as in the case of the environmental legislation of the early 1970s, available technical and scientific knowledge may be insufficient to indicate ways that unambiguously fulfill the original goals. Because uncertainty is so pervasive in policy-making, the values of administrators and experts inevitably count a great deal.

Hence, in drawing the conceptual distinction between norm setting or policy-making on the one hand, and norm using or administration on the other, we must be careful to avoid any implication that policy and administration occupy two completely separate spheres, or are the responsibility of two completely separate groups of people. Norm setting is not the prerogative of high-level policymakers, nor do administrators and experts deal only with means. In fact, as Charles W. Anderson writes,

> the actual role of policy professionalism in contemporary government is probably more prescriptive than instrumental. The setting of standards of good practice is a large part of what professionalism means. Most policy professions are such precisely because they provide standards for public policy. In such diverse fields as forestry, public health, nutrition and welfare, the essential function of the expert is often that of setting criteria for the definition of public objectives and the appraisal of public programs.[7]

Experts may play an important role in setting standards for public policy even when they appear to be dealing with purely factual questions. The following example is typical of a wide

7. "The Place of Principles in Policy Analysis," *The American Political Science Review* 73, no. 3 (Sept. 1979): 714.

range of situations in regulatory decision making.[8] In 1974 an environmental group, the Environmental Defense Fund, petitioned the Environmental Protection Agency (EPA) to suspend and cancel two chemical pesticides, Aldrin and Dieldrin (A/D). During the cancellation hearings it became clear that there was no agreement over the standards for inferring carcinogenicity. The experts for Shell Chemical Company, the producer of A/D, argued that certain strict criteria had to be satisfied before a substance could be considered to be carcinogenic. The standards advocated by these experts included traditional toxicologic criteria such as the development of tumors in two or more animal species exposed to the substance in the laboratory, proof that the tumors are substance-related, and the availability of data proving the existence of at least one human cancer. EPA's case against A/D rested on different criteria of carcinogenicity. According to the agency's experts, a carcinogen is any agent that increases the induction of even benign tumors in people or animals; a carcinogenic agent may be identified through analysis of experiments on animals or on the basis of properly conducted epidemiological studies; and any substance that produces tumors in one animal species in appropriately conducted tests must be considered a carcinogenic hazard to man.

Neither set of criteria could be dismissed as being unreasonable or contrary to the rules of scientific evidence. Consequently, the choice had to be made on nonscientific grounds. In objecting to Shell's criterion of at least one A/D-induced human cancer, the EPA's experts maintained that since animal tests were sufficient to predict carcinogenic risk, it was ethically unjustifiable to wait for the demonstration of human harm. They also argued that the dictates of prudent policy implied that positive evidence of tumors in one animal species should supersede negative results in other species.

In advocating standards of evidence that departed significantly from more traditional toxicologic criteria, the EPA's ex-

8. A full discussion of this example can be found in Brendan Gillespie, Dave Eva, and Ron Johnston, "Carcinogenic Risk Assessment in the United States and Great Britain: The Case of Aldrin/Dieldrin," *Social Studies of Science* 9 (1979): 265–302.

perts were effectively proposing new norms for public policy concerning carcinogenic risk, including criteria of what constitutes sufficient evidence for public decisions. The general lesson suggested by this and previous examples is clear. Experts, including policy analysts, are often engaged in setting norms rather than in searching for solutions that satisfy given norms. Empirical methods have no point of attack until there is agreement on norms, since the nature of the problem depends on which norms are adopted. Hence, argument and persuasion play the key role in norm setting and problem definition.

Similar conclusions hold in the case of policy evaluation, as I will show in more detail in chapter 8. The prominence achieved by evaluation research in recent years shows that policy analysts have finally come to realize that the effective delivery of public services requires more than the discovery and installation of some theoretically optimal program. Even more important is to learn how the program actually behaves, whether it is accomplishing what was intended, and if not, how it can be improved or discontinued.

It is widely assumed that these are purely empirical determinations, involving neither value choices nor preconceived opinions. In fact, values and opinions count for a great deal in evaluation partly because the outcomes of practice are intrinsically ambiguous under normal circumstances. Data are often poor and the measurement instruments unreliable; in addition, the causes of both success and failure are multiple, and different stakeholders are usually interested in singling out some particular subset of causes. Hence, the assessment of a particular outcome depends on which assumptions and criteria the evaluator adopts. The profound equivocality of praxis, to use Donald Campbell's phrase,[9] cannot be removed by improved measurement and testing techniques, but can be represented and clarified in argumentation and reciprocal persuasion.

    9. "Experiments as Arguments," *Knowledge: Creation, Diffusion, Utilization* 3, no. 3 (March 1982): 327–37.

DISCOVERY AND JUSTIFICATION

When analyzing policy decisions, or decision processes in general, it is useful to distinguish between the procedure by which a conclusion is reached—the process of discovery—and the procedure by which the conclusion may be justified—the process of justification. The way in which a conclusion was reached does not always answer the question of whether the conclusion is in fact reasonable or justifiable. For example, the personal motives that guided the decision maker may be inadequate to explain his decision to others or to persuade them to implement it. If we term those considerations on which a person acts *motives* and those which may be used in interpersonal communication *reasons,* then we may say that not all motives need be reasons and that not all reasons function as motives.[10]

Similarly, the way a solution to a mathematical or scientific problem is discovered is not always or even usually the way in which the solution is presented, justified, or defended to the community of specialists. Even in scientific problem solving the private moment of intuition must be followed by a public process of justification and persuasion.

The distinction between motives and reasons, or between discovery and justification, is not sufficiently appreciated by analysts and other students of policy-making, but its significance has been clearly recognized by legal scholars and philosophers of science. Consider the case of a judge who decides a case on the basis of his subjective notion of fairness, a hunch that a particular decision would be right, while realizing at the same time that considerations of this kind do not count as justifications for a binding determination. Thus, the judge frames his opinion in the objective categories of legal argument, and any subsequent developments in the case (for example, an appeal) will be based on the published opinion, not on the actual process followed by the judge in coming to the conclusion. It is a fact of great methodological interest that most legal systems allow the opinion stat-

10. David P. Gauthier, *Practical Reasoning* (Oxford: Oxford University Press, 1963), 17–18.

ing the reasons for a judicial decision to follow rather than precede that decision. Also, different judges may agree on a decision but disagree about the best way to justify it; in the American system they are given the opportunity to present their positions in separate arguments.

Such procedural rules must seem absurd to somebody who assumes that a judicial opinion is an accurate description of the decision process followed by the judge in coming to a conclusion. If, however, the opinion is viewed as a report of justificatory procedures employed by the judge, then the appeal to legal and logical considerations, which possibly played no role in the actual decision process, becomes quite understandable.[11] In fact, the judge's opinion is not the premise of a syllogism that concludes in the decision; it is, rather, a means of increasing the persuasive force of the decision and exercising rational control over conclusions that may be suggested by extralegal considerations.

Contrary to what positivism would have us believe, justificatory arguments also play an important role in science. Scientific arguments, it is now recognized, are attempts to make some theory extremely plausible and convincing, but cannot be conclusively proved either by mathematics or by inductive procedures. In the words of physicist John Ziman, scientific reports "are not diaries or journals, telling us exactly what occurred in a particular laboratory on a particular day. They give, rather, a carefully edited version of such events, and inform us what ought to happen if you try to repeat the experiment yourself under the prescribed conditions."[12] The communication of the experimenter to his colleagues is not merely an exposition of what happened when certain operations were performed; rather, it is an attempt to convince them that the world behaves as the scientist has conceived it. After the private moment of discovery, "there must come the public demonstration, the deliberate process of persuasion. That is why I say that a good experiment is a powerful piece of rhetoric; it has the ability to persuade the

11. Richard A. Wasserstrom, *The Judicial Decision* (Stanford, Cal.: Stanford University Press, 1961), 28.

12. *Public Knowledge* (Cambridge: Cambridge University Press, 1968), 35.

most obdurate and skeptical mind to accept a new idea; it makes a positive contribution to public knowledge."[13]

Justificatory arguments play an even larger role in policy-making. To decide, even to decide correctly, is never enough in politics. Decisions must be legitimated, accepted, and carried out. After the moment of choice comes the process of justification, explanation, and persuasion. Also, policymakers often act in accordance with pressures from external events or the force of personal convictions. In such cases arguments are needed *after* the decision is made to provide a conceptual basis for it, to show that it fits into the framework of existing policy, to increase assent, to discover new implications, and to anticipate or answer criticism.

Moreover, since policies exist for some time, their political support must be continuously renewed and new arguments are constantly needed to give the different policy components the greatest possible internal coherence and the closest fit to an ever-changing environment. Policy development does not consist of taking first this decision and then that, piecemeal. Rather, as I will argue in chapter 7, the process of policy development is guided by a parallel intellectual process of refining and developing some original policy idea.

Thus, postdecision arguments are indispensable in policy-making, yet they have been traditionally dismissed as attempts at "rationalization." Indeed, one of the recurring criticisms of analysis is that it provides "pseudo-scientific rationalizations" for politically or bureaucratically determined positions. For example, it was said that Robert McNamara, the former U.S. secretary of defense, used "studies showing greater cost-effectiveness for passive rather than active defense . . . as ammunition against congressmen who wanted [the antiballistic missile], even though McNamara's opposition to ABM was based on other factors."[14]

Whether or not this particular allegation is true, it is not necessarily dishonest or merely "rationalizing" to use arguments

13. Ibid., 36.
14. Charles A. Murdock, *Defense Policy Formation* (Syracuse, N.Y.: Syracuse University Press, 1974), 95.

based on considerations different from those that led to the
adoption of a certain position. We have already emphasized the
fact that arguments are not formal proofs. A logical or mathematical proof is either true or false; if it is true, then it automatically wins the assent of any person able to understand it.
Arguments are only more or less plausible, more or less convincing to a particular audience. It has also been pointed out
that there is no unique way to construct an argument: data and
evidence can be selected in a wide variety of ways from the
available information, and there are several alternative methods
of analysis and ways of ordering values. Hence, there is nothing
intrinsically reprehensible in selecting the particular combination of facts, values, and methods that seems to be most appropriate to convince a particular audience.

The importance of postdecision arguments for rationalizing
actions and guiding policy development is particularly evident
in economic policy-making. For example, President Franklin D.
Roosevelt's policy of increased government spending to reduce
unemployment and get out of the depression has been called
Keynesian. But Roosevelt did not have to learn about government spending from Keynes. The idea that the influence of the
British economist lay behind the policies of the New Deal began
to take root fairly early, but it is only a legend.[15] The theories
of Keynes merely provided a sophisticated rationale for what
Roosevelt was doing anyway. The answers that these theories
provided to questions about the causes of long-term unemployment and the reasons for the effectiveness of public spending
were not prerequisites for Roosevelt's expansionist fiscal policy.
But as these answers came to dominate the thinking of economists and politicians, they helped to make expansionist fiscal
policy the core idea of liberal economic policy for several decades. In the words of Herbert Stein, a former chairman of the
President's Council of Economic Advisers, "Without Keynes, and
especially without the interpretation of Keynes by his followers,

15. Donald Winch, *Economics and Policy* (London: Hodder and Stoughton,
1969), 219–22.

expansionist fiscal policy might have remained an occasional emergency measure and not become a way of life."[16]

Thus, it is wrong to assume that the only legitimate use of analysis is to assist the policymaker in discovering a solution to a problem. Policymakers need retrospective (postdecision) analysis at least as much as they need prospective (or predecision) analysis, and probably more. That this kind of analysis is shunned by many analysts can only be explained by the constraining hold of the decisionist methodology on their minds. As I argued in chapter 1, a serious limitation of this methodology is precisely its failure to appreciate the significance of the rhetorical aspects of policy-making—the role of justification, communication, and persuasion in the formation and development of public policy.

The fundamental reason for failing to appreciate these aspects of policy-making is now clear. As long as rationality is defined as choosing the best means to a given end, it is natural to consider retrospective justificatory arguments as being outside the pale of professional analysis—"mere rhetoric," propaganda, or rationalization. However, this instrumental view is not an adequate characterization of the role of reason in human affairs. The social psychologist Karl E. Weick has made the point with particular cogency:

> Rationality makes sense of what has been, not what will be. It is a process of justification in which past deeds are made to appear sensible to the actor himself and to those other persons to whom he feels accountable. It is difficult for a person to be rational if he does not know precisely what it is that he must be rational about. He can create rationality only when he has available some set of actions which can be viewed in several ways. It is possible for actors to make elaborate, detailed statements of their plans. However, the error comes if we assume that these plans then control their behavior. If we watch closely, it will become clear that the behavior is under the control of more determinants than just the vocally stated plan. And at the conclusion of the actions, it will never be true that the plan as first stated will have been

16. *Presidential Economics* (New York: Simon and Schuster, 1984), 39.

exactly accomplished. But something will have been accomplished, and it is this something, and the making sense of this something, that constitute rationality.[17]

Thus, modern psychological theory reinstates the classic notion of rationality: an action is rational if it can be explained and defended by arguments acceptable to a reasonable audience. In this old-new perspective any sharp distinction between discovery and justification, or between reasons and rationalizations, appears artificial and unrealistic.

ADVOCACY

Equally artificial and difficult to sustain in practice is the related distinction between policy analysis and policy advocacy—between laying out the alternatives that can accomplish a given goal and advocating changes in what governments do. Analysts with extensive experience in advising policymakers in business and government point out that clients want and need advice about objectives as well as the most efficient ways of achieving them.

Economist Carl Kaysen goes as far as arguing that in his role as adviser, the economist "functions primarily as a propagandist of values, not as a technician supplying data for the pre-existing preferences of the policy makers.... The adviser becomes, in fact, a supplier of arguments and briefs which seek to gain wider support for economists' political values."[18] This is an extreme opinion with which few economists or other social scientists would agree, but it is the understandable reaction of a practicing analyst caught between the impossible demands of an outdated methodology and a widespread unwillingness to discuss openly the rhetorical aspects of his craft.

The prevailing positivistic methodology of the social sciences

17. *The Social Psychology of Organizing* (Reading, Mass.: Addison-Wesley, 1969), 38.

18. "Model-Makers and Decision-Makers: Economists and the Policy Process," *Public Interest* 12 (Summer 1968): 83.

stresses the separation of facts from values and prizes objectivity and a willingness to report findings whether or not they agree with one's preferences or expectations. But as we said earlier, values and preferences are shaped by experiences; the choice of means helps to alter the criteria by which the correctness of the means must be judged. Although people consider what to do before they act, they act in the light of what they are already doing and of what is presently happening. The analyst cannot bring the policy process to a stop while goals are defined and values clarified, and then set everything once more in motion.

Moreover, the findings of social science are usually open to a variety of explanations and interpretations. Like the issues of regulatory science mentioned in chapter 1, many questions investigated by social scientists are trans-scientific in the sense that they can be stated in the language of science but cannot be answered in strictly scientific terms. Few theories advanced by social scientists can be tested by means of controlled experiments. At any rate, it would be too expensive and time-consuming to generate the kinds of data required to refute the various theories proposed on such issues as the causes and possible remedies of crime and illiteracy, the relation between education and earnings, or that between employment and inflation. Hence, any particular set of facts will be consistent with a variety of theories and hypotheses.[19] Since the official methodology provides no objective criterion for choosing under these circumstances, analysts cannot be blamed for selecting the explanation that best fits their preconceived opinions or expectations. The fault lies not in using subjective criteria but in leaving those criteria unexamined.

In addition, the job of the analyst is not only to find solutions within given constraints, but also to push out the boundaries of the possible in public policy. Major policy breakthroughs become possible only after public opinion has been persuaded to accept new ideas. But new ideas face powerful intellectual and institutional obstacles. Economic, bureaucratic, and political interests combine to restrict the range of options that are submitted to

19. Aaron, *Politics and the Professor*, 164–67.

Kingdom

public deliberation or given serious consideration by the experts. Because of intellectual and institutional inertia, ideas in agreement with current practices and accepted doctrine usually enjoy a considerable comparative advantage over unconventional proposals. At the same time, new ideas generally lack strong empirical and theoretical support. Time is needed until favorable evidence accumulates and auxiliary theories come to the rescue. For all these reasons, objective analysis, unassisted by advocacy and persuasion, is seldom sufficient to achieve major policy innovations.

Thus, in order to be effective, an analyst must often be an advocate as well. But he is also a firm believer in the virtues of the scientific method, and this belief is generally associated with a distaste for advocacy and persuasion. One way to defuse the conflict between practical effectiveness and scientific integrity is to note that many outstanding scientists have not been loath to use persuasion when the situation seemed to require it. For example, eminent historians of science like Duhem and Koyré have likened the work of Galileo to propaganda. "But propaganda of this kind is not a marginal affair that may or may not be added to allegedly more substantial means of defense, and that should perhaps be avoided by the 'professionally honest scientist.' In the circumstances we are considering now, *propaganda is of the essence*. It is of the essence because interest must be created at a time when the usual methodological prescriptions have no point of attack; and because this interest must be maintained, perhaps for centuries, until new reasons arrive."[20]

As one would expect, the role of persuasion is even more significant in the social sciences. Thus, in discussing Adam Smith's principles of division of labor and free exchange, the authors of a well-known textbook on economics write: "It is interesting that Smith's book did not contain a logically correct exposition; instead it contained a masterfully persuasive statement of the results of free exchange. It was Robert Torrens who, some forty years after the idea had been 'sold,' demonstrated its logical validity. Possibly, had Smith tried to give a logically air-

20. Paul Feyerabend, *Against Method* (London: NLB, 1975), 52.

See McCloskey

tight demonstration, instead of a suggestive, plausible interpretation, he would never have made his 'point' popular."[21] George Stigler adds Jevons and Böhm-Bawerk to the list of outstanding economists who "have employed the techniques of the huckster." According to Stigler, persuasive arguments have preceded and accompanied the adoption on a large scale of almost every idea in economic theory.[22]

If advocacy and persuasion play such an important role in the development of scientific ideas, can policy analysts afford to slight them in the name of a historically mistaken view of scientific method? In policy analysis, as in science and in everyday reasoning, few arguments are purely rational or purely persuasive. A careful blend of reason and persuasion is usually more effective than exclusive reliance on one or the other. Style, elegance of expression, and novel modes of communication are often important means of winning support for a new idea and overcoming preconceived hostility and institutional inertia. The practical question, therefore, is not whether to use persuasion, but which form of persuasion to use and when. There are in fact, as we shall see in a moment, situations where the use of persuasion, far from violating the analyst's code of professional behavior, is not only effective but also rationally and ethically justifiable.

ADVICE AND PERSUASION

To examine in more detail the role of persuasion in analysis, let us consider the important special case of policy advice. Advice is sought and given in different situations depending, among other things, on the clarity of the objectives of the policymaker, his understanding of the problem situation, and the knowledge

21. Armen A. Alchian and W. R. Allen, *University Economics* (London: Prentice-Hall International, 1974), 211.

22. *Essays in the History of Economics* (Chicago: University of Chicago Press, 1965), 5.

and stance of the adviser. Three situations deserve to be singled out for special attention.[23]

In the first situation, the task of the adviser is to determine the best, cheapest, or most effective way of achieving an objective that the policymaker has already decided to aim at. Here the advice takes the form "If you want A, then do B," as in the economist's prescription "If you want to maximize profits, set production at the level where marginal revenue equals marginal cost." The assumption implicit in such prescriptions is that the problem has a definite solution and that there exists a well-defined procedure which, if followed, will enable the advisee to achieve his objectives. In other words, the advisee's goal is clear and the path to it is also clear, though not to the advisee; the analyst only needs to work out the answer. Recommendations made in situations of this type are better described as instructions or prescriptions than as advice.

We meet a somewhat different situation when the policy-maker's problem involves more than selection of the most appropriate means to achieve a given end. For example, the policymaker may be uncertain about the nature of the problem to be solved; he feels that things are not as they should be, but has no clear idea about what should be done. Even when the problem situation is reasonably well defined there may be several alternative formulations or methods of solution but no standard way of choosing among them. In such cases, which are quite frequent in practice, it is appropriate to say that the analyst gives advice rather than instructions or prescriptions, as in the first case.

Finally, we may identify a third type of situation in which the analyst uses the language of advice to redirect the policymaker's attitudes, preferences, or cognitive beliefs. If, for example, the analyst feels that the policymaker has incorrectly formulated the problem, he may feel obliged to persuade him to accept his (the analyst's) formulation. In such cases, one should perhaps speak of persuasive advice; the question is, under what circumstances is this form of advice rationally and morally justifiable? Notice that when the analyst uses persuasion, he is always acting, at least in part, as advocate rather than disinterested adviser.

Sometimes persuasion is a necessary preliminary to get the policymaker's or the public's attention, to make them "listen to reason" when they are blinded by stereotypes or by wishful thinking. Walter Heller, a former chairman of the Council of Economic Advisers, gives this example: "In 1961, with over five million unemployed and a production gap of nearly $50 billion, the problem of the economic adviser was not what to say, but how to get people to listen. Even the President could not adopt modern economic advice, however golden, as long as the Congress and the public 'knew' that it was only fool's gold.... Men's minds had to be conditioned to accept new thinking, new symbols, and new and broader concepts of the public interest."[24] As Heller suggests, policymakers tend to think in traditional categories, or in terms of alternatives that are unduly restricted in relation to their own objectives. Persuasion is needed to induce them to consider different formulations or approaches to the issue under discussion since the psychological effect of factual arguments may not be strong enough to overcome the inertia of long-established patterns of thought. Experience also shows that facts and statistics are seldom sufficient to bring about changes in behavior—even after the need for a change has become clear. For this reason, public policies to induce citizens to adopt healthier lifestyles tend to rely at least as much on persuasion as on objective information.

Next consider the case where the motivation to attack a persistent problem, such as crime or illiteracy, is in advance of the knowledge required to solve it. It may be that the technical tools for an adequate treatment of the problem do not yet exist, or that good evidence on causal factors is hard to get. In such cases popular appeals and persuasion, bolstered by whatever empirical and theoretical knowledge is available, may succeed in stimulating interest in the issue and keeping it alive until satisfactory methods of solution have been developed.

24. *New Dimensions of Political Economy* (New York: W. W. Norton, 1967), 27.

When knowledge of a problem is very limited, experts tend to disagree about its causes and possible solutions and are thus unable to provide unequivocal advice. In this situation it is usually better to let each expert openly advocate his position, preferably in a well-structured adversary setting, than to attempt to enforce a consensus in the name of scientific objectivity. Adversary procedures are specifically designed to bring out unstated assumptions, differing interpretations of the facts, and gaps in logic or in the evidence. Thus, they provide powerful incentives for the adversaries to present the strongest arguments in favor of their respective positions.

Because of these advantages, the adversary process, in a form called "multiple advocacy," has been recommended as a way of organizing expert advice in areas of public policy such as national security and economic policy-making at the presidential level. The basic assumption underlying multiple advocacy is that a competition of ideas and viewpoints, rather than reliance on analyses and recommendations from advisers who share the perspective of the policymaker, is the best method of developing policy. Multiple advocacy is a process of debate and persuasion designed to expose the policymaker systematically to competing arguments made by the advocates themselves. Through the offices of an "honest broker" it attempts to ensure that all interested parties are represented in genuinely adversarial roles, and that the debate is structured and balanced.[25]

In all the cases we have discussed, persuasion is justifiable on professional as well as ethical grounds. It is also important to keep in mind that since policy analysis cannot produce conclusive proofs but only more or less convincing arguments, persuasion always has a role to play in increasing both the acceptability of advice and the willingness to act on less than complete evidence. For this reason, experienced analysts suggest that analysis should be done in two stages: the first stage to find out what the analyst wants to recommend, and a second stage to make the recom-

25. Roger B. Porter, *Presidential Decision Making* (Cambridge: Cambridge University Press, 1980); Alexander L. George, "The Case for Multiple Advocacy in Making Foreign Policy," *American Political Science Review* 66 (Sept. 1972): 751–85.

mendation convincing even to a hostile and disbelieving audience.[26] This is sound advice as long as it is not interpreted to imply that communication and persuasion are discrete and separable parts of analysis rather than pervasive aspects of the analytic process.

Throughout this chapter I have emphasized that in order to be persuasive, evidence and arguments must be chosen with a particular audience in mind: the same conclusions may have to be justified differently in different contexts.

As Arnold Meltsner points out in an interesting essay on communication in policy analysis, concentrating on the immediate client as the sole recipient of advice and information may be dangerous.[27] In a complex organization or political system, the immediate client is only one of numerous actors who comprise the analyst's audience, and the analyst may be mistaken in focusing his communication on that single client. Too, it is often difficult to prevent the dissemination of analytic information through press reports, public debate, or deliberate leaks. In principle, any reader of a policy study may be considered a member of the analyst's audience. Finally, it is possible that by the time the analysis is completed, the original client will have been replaced, key elected and appointed officials will have left office, and other actors will have moved on to another problem.

For all these reasons, *audience*—a term with a long tradition in rhetoric—is a better, more flexible, and more neutral characterization of the set of actual or potential recipients and users of analysis than more familiar terms like *client* or *decision maker*. It also reminds us that the main justification of advocacy and persuasion in democratic policy-making is their function in a continuous process of mutual learning through discourse.

26. Hermann Kahn and Igor Mann, *Techniques of Systems Analysis* (Santa Monica, Calif.: Rand Corporation, RM–1829, Dec. 1956).

27. "Don't Slight Communication: Some Problems of Analytical Practice," in Giandomenico Majone and Edward S. Quade, eds., *Pitfalls of Analysis* (New York: Wiley, 1980), 116–37.

THREE

Analysis as Craft

The argumentative model of analysis assumes that analysts can seldom demonstrate the correctness of their conclusions, but only produce more or less persuasive evidence and reasonable arguments. However, belief in the possibility of discovering correct solutions for a wide variety of problems has been important historically in legitimating the use of analysis in policy-making. Hence, the admission that analysis is fallible raises professional as well as political questions. First, is it at all possible to define standards of quality for policy analysis if its conclusions are always tentative and open to refutation? Or, to put the same question in a slightly different form, how can analysts steer a safe course between the Scylla of absolute certainty and the Charybdis of methodological anarchism—the easy philosophy of "anything goes"? Finally, how can policy analysis be justified and legitimated once the claim to certainty of conclusions is abandoned?

This chapter provides some answers to these questions by looking at the craft aspects of analysis, the details of the process by which policy arguments are produced. My approach reflects recent developments in the philosophy and sociology of science.

Few scientists and philosophers of science still believe that scientific knowledge is, or can be, proven knowledge. If there is one point on which all schools of thought agree today, it is that scientific knowledge is always tentative and open to refutation. And while the older history of science was little more than a chronicle of the irresistible advance of the different sciences, the contemporary historian tries to understand "how such sciences can succeed in fulfilling their actual explanatory missions, despite the fact that, at any chosen moment in time, their intellectual contents are marked by logical gaps, incoherences, and contradictions."[1] Even mathematical knowledge is fallible, tentative, and evolving, as is every other kind of human knowledge.[2]

Since the endeavors of individual scientists are fallible, the emergence of a (provisionally) accepted body of knowledge must be explained in terms of social mechanisms of evaluation and quality control. "Nature," writes Jerome Ravetz, "is not so obliging as ever to give marks of True and False for scientific work, and so a scientific community sets its standards for itself."[3]

As contemporary epistemologists emphasize, some form of conventionalism is the inescapable logical consequence of fallibilism. If there is no demonstrative certainty for the conclusions of science, their "truth," or at any rate their acceptability as scientific results, can only be established by convention: through a consensus of experts in the field and the fulfillment of certain methodological and professional norms—the rules of the scientific game.

In planning an experiment, evaluating a batch of data, or choosing among alternative research strategies, the scientist utilizes knowledge and skills that are not themselves scientific but are acquired by practice and imitation. In the language of chapter 1, the process of scientific research (as distinct from the fin-

1. Stephen Toulmin, "The Structure of Scientific Theories," in Frederick Suppe, ed., *The Structure of Scientific Theories*, 2d ed. (Urbana, Ill.: University of Illinois Press, 1977), 605.

2. Philip J. Davis and Reuben Hersh, *The Mathematical Experience* (Boston: Houghton, Mifflin, 1981), 406.

3. *Scientific Knowledge and Its Social Problems* (Harmondsworth, England: Penguin, 1973), 82.

ished products of research) depends more on "knowing how" than "knowing that"; it is a craft, a social process, rather than a purely logical activity.

The craft skills of the scientist form a repertoire of procedures and judgments that are partly personal, partly social and institutional. Thus, in deciding whether a batch of data is of acceptable quality, the scientist applies standards that derive from his own experience but also reflect the professional norms of teachers and colleagues, as well as culturally and institutionally determined criteria of adequacy. Because of the concentration of the older philosophy of science on the logical status of achieved scientific knowledge, the craft aspects of scientific investigation have been neglected until recently. Yet without an appreciation of such aspects "there is no possibility of resolving the paradox of the radical difference between the subjective, intensely personal activity of creative science, and the objective, impersonal knowledge which results from it."[4]

THE ANALYST AS CRAFTSMAN

Craft knowledge—less general and explicit than theoretical knowledge, but not as idiosyncratic as pure intuition—is essential in any kind of disciplined intellectual inquiry or professional activity. It is especially important in policy analysis. The structure of an analytic argument is typically a complex blend of factual propositions, logical deductions, evaluations, and recommendations. Along with mathematical and logical arguments it includes statistical inferences, references to previous studies and to expert opinion, value judgments, and caveats and provisos of different kinds. As we remarked before, this unavoidable complexity rules out the possibility of any formal testing—of proving or refuting the final conclusions. Whatever testing can be done will have to use a variety of criteria derived from craft experience, including the special features of the problem, the quality of the data, the limitations of the available tools, and the re-

4. Ibid., 75.

quirements of the audience. Only a detailed examination of the different components of the task of the analyst qua craftsman can help the producer or user of analysis steer a reasonable course between unhelpful counsels of perfection and methodological anarchism.

The common-sense notion of craft includes, as basic elements, a body of skills that can be used to produce useful objects; careful attention to the quality of the product; and a sense of responsibility both to the ends of the client and to the values of the guild.[5] In light of these characteristics, to speak of the analyst as a craftsman is actually more than merely using a metaphor: the similarity between the work of the analyst and that of the traditional craftsman is real. In policy analysis, as in the traditional crafts, successful performance depends crucially on an intimate knowledge of materials and tools, and on a highly personal relationship between the agent and his task. Good analytic work cannot be produced mechanically any more than handicraft can be mass-produced. Style can play as big a role in determining the value and acceptability of the analytic product as it does for the results of the craftsman's work.

There are, of course, obvious differences. The craftsman uses concrete materials in order to produce an object that has an appropriate shape and fulfills a specific function. The analyst, on the other hand, operates with concepts, theories, data, and technical tools to produce arguments and evidence in support of certain conclusions. In spite of these differences, craftsmanship is an essential element of any skillful performance. In fact, the classical Aristotelian analysis of craft work has been usefully applied to scientific inquiry[6] and will be shown to be relevant also to a discussion of the anatomy of the analyst's task.

Aristotle's scheme involves four constituents (or "causes") of the craftsman's task: material, efficient, formal, and final. They refer, respectively, to the physical substance that is worked on; to the tools the craftsman uses in shaping it; to the form or shape

5. Howard S. Becker, "Arts and Crafts," *American Journal of Sociology* 83, no. 4 (1978): 862–89; Robert T. Holt and John E. Turner, "The Scholar as Artisan," *Policy Sciences* 5 (1974): 257–70.
6. Ravetz, *Scientific Knowledge*, chap. 3.

acquired by the substance; and to the purpose of the activity—
the creation of an object that fulfills certain functions. To adapt
this scheme to the analyst's work, the material component should
be identified with the data and information that are used in
defining the problem. Tools and techniques are the efficient
component of the analyst's task. The "form" of the task is an
argument in which evidence is cited and from which a conclusion
is drawn, while the final component is the conclusion itself, with
the related activities of communication and implementation.

This description of the analyst's task enjoys some advantages
over more familiar descriptions. For example, the categories
suggested by the decision-making approach (goals, alternatives,
consequences, criteria of choice) focus attention on a rather
narrow use of analysis in choice-making situations. The craft
paradigm, on the other hand, provides categories—data, information, tools, evidence, arguments, conclusions—that are applicable to any type and style of analysis, prospective or
retrospective, descriptive or prescriptive, or in an advocacy
mode. In turn, these categories clarify important but often overlooked distinctions and, at the same time, facilitate the critical
appraisal of the different stages of the analytic process.

DATA, INFORMATION, EVIDENCE

By way of example and as a first application of the craft paradigm, I shall elaborate the distinction already made in chapter
1 among data, information, and evidence. These terms are often
used interchangeably with unfortunate consequences not only
for the clarity of discourse but, more importantly, for our ability
to evaluate the quality of policy arguments.

Data are, so to speak, the raw materials necessary for the
investigation of a problem, or perhaps the result of the first
working-up of such materials. In policy analysis data are often
"found" rather than "manufactured"; that is, they are obtained
by unplanned observations (as in the case of a time series) rather
than by planned experiments. This fact, as will be shown in the

next section dealing with pitfalls, requires craft skills that are rather different from, and in many respects more difficult to acquire than, those needed for the analysis of experimental data.

When data are obtained by sampling, the sampling process may be influenced by the method used, the skill of the sampler, and a host of other factors that could lead to results quite unrepresentative of the general situation. Also, data are usually collected according to categorical descriptions that seldom fit perfectly the purposes of any given inquiry. Even when data are produced by experiments, as in the case of some large-scale social experiments conducted in the United States, there is no guarantee that the best experimental design offers sufficient protection against dangers and pitfalls, of which the "Hawthorne effect"—the fact that people may behave differently when they know they are observed—is only one of the best-known examples.

In sum, since perfection of data is impossible, the standards of acceptance will have to be based on craft judgments of what is good enough for the functions the data perform in a particular problem. Such judgments depend both on internal, disciplinary criteria and on criteria related to the nature of the problem: the standards of adequacy applicable to problems of monetary policy, say, are not necessarily relevant to problems arising in education or welfare. Thus, the simple judgment of soundness of data reveals as in a microcosm all the personal judgments and accumulated institutional experience that go into analytic work.

Before being used in an argument, data usually have to be refined into a more useful and reliable form. This transformation of data involves a new set of craft skills, the application of new tools (often of a statistical or mathematical nature), and the making of a new set of judgments. This new phase of the analyst's work, the production of information, can be illustrated by a variety of examples: the calculation of averages and other statistical indices and parameters, the fitting of a curve to a set of points, the reduction of data by means of some multivariate statistical technique. The operations performed on the original data may be involved or quite simple, but they always represent a crucial step. Through these operations the raw data have been transformed into a new sort of material, and from this point on the analysis is carried out only in terms of these new entities.

Evidence, as the term is used here, is not the same as *data* or *information*. It is, rather, information selected from the available stock and introduced at a specific point in an argument "to persuade the mind that a given factual proposition is true or false."[7] As previously noted, an inappropriate choice of data, their placement at a wrong point in the argument, a style of presentation that is unsuitable for the audience to which the argument is directed—any one of these factors can destroy the effectiveness of information as evidence, regardless of its intrinsic cognitive content. Hence, the criteria for asssessing evidence are different from those applicable to "facts." While facts can be evaluated by more or less objective tests, the acceptability of evidence depends on a number of features peculiar to a given situation, such as the nature of the case, the type of audience, the prevailing "rules of evidence," and even the persuasiveness of the analyst.

Similarly, the assessment of the strength and fit of the evidence is considerably more complicated than judgments about the validity and reliability of data. For this reason disputes often arise about the acceptability of the conclusions of policy studies—disputes that cannot be settled either by examination of the data and information or by an appeal to accepted criteria of adequacy. The point that Frederick Mosteller and Daniel P. Moynihan make about the 1966 *Report on Equality of Education Opportunity* (the so-called Coleman Report) has general relevance: "Professional judgments were made in the survey design and analysis that are open to dispute. This is not always a matter of being right or wrong, but simply of the absence of professional consensus on the points involved."[8]

The special significance of evidence is most easily recognized in fields such as law and history, where problems involve both complex arguments and large masses of data, but where the

7. See s.v. "Evidence" in *Encyclopedia Britannica*, 15th ed. (Chicago, 1974), 8: 905.

8. Frederick Mosteller and Daniel P. Moynihan, eds., *On Equality of Educational Opportunity* (New York: Random House, 1972), 32.

reliability and relevance of the information cannot easily be assessed by standard methods. Thus, in jurisprudence we find a highly developed "law of evidence" for the presentation and testing of information offered as evidence in court cases. Judicial notice, facts, documents, physical evidence, testimonial evidence, and hearsay are carefully distinguished and subject to different procedural rules—rules that attempt to balance the value of information against the cost of obtaining it.

Similarly, budding historians are taught to distinguish between records (intentional transmitters of facts) and relics (unpremeditated transmitters of facts), between written and oral testimony, archaeological and linguistic evidence, and so on. Faced with a piece of evidence, the historian asks: Is this object or document genuine? Who is its author or maker? How does the statement compare with other statements on the same point? What do we know independently about the author and his or her credibility?[9]

Problems of evidence are discussed at length in several modern classics of historical methodology. Books like E. H. Carr's *What Is History?*, Marc Bloch's *Historian's Craft*, and Robin Winks's *Historian as Detective*[10] are rich in insights whose relevance goes well beyond historical scholarship. They are particularly relevant for policy analysts, who are also constantly faced with problems of evidence. Consider, for example, the problem posed to the analyst by the fact that policy actors will often give different accounts of some crucial event—so different, in fact, that it is almost inconceivable that everyone was perceiving the same event.[11]

Why, then, has the literature of policy analysis practically ignored problems of evidence, except for some recent discussions

9. Jacques Barzun and Henry F. Graff, *The Modern Researcher* (New York: Harcourt, Brace, and World, 1957), 131–53.

10. Edward Hallett Carr, *What is History?* (New York: Random House, 1961); Marc Bloch, *The Historian's Craft* (New York: Alfred A. Knopf, 1953); Robin W. Winks, ed., *The Historian as Detective: Essays on Evidence* (New York: Harper and Row, 1970).

11. Charles O. Jones, *An Introduction to the Study of Public Policy*, 2d ed. (North Scituate, Mass.: Duxbury, 1977), 1–13.

on the use of statistical evidence in policy-making?[12] One reason
has already been alluded to in chapter 1: the intellectualist bias
of decisionism, with its emphasis on "knowing that" rather than
"knowing how," has led to a general neglect of the craft aspects
of policy analysis, including the skills necessary for a critical
evaluation of evidence. In turn, this bias is related to the positivistic tradition in the philosophy of science. Being mainly concerned with the logical and epistemological problems of achieved
knowledge, this school has paid very little attention to the actual
processes of the production of scientific knowledge.

In this, as in other cases, uncritical acceptance of the "scientific
method" (or what is thought to be the scientific method) overlooks some important differences between the natural sciences
and policy analysis. For if it is true that neither descriptive nor
theoretical natural sciences require highly developed skills in
testing evidence, beyond those already involved in producing
information, this is for good reasons. In the natural sciences one
usually has either a rich and reliable body of information with
a relatively simple argument, or a complex theoretical argument
needing evidence at only a few points.[13] Such situations are
rather exceptional in policy analysis, where one typically deals
with large amounts of data of doubtful reliability or relevance.
It is likely that the lack of suitable rules of evidence has contributed to the mounting level of dissatisfaction with certain applications of policy analysis.

In particular, large-scale, policy-oriented models have come
under heavy attack in recent years. Examples of conceptual,
technical, and institutional pitfalls in model construction and
utilization have been given in a number of review papers and
book-length case studies, leading some critics to conclude that
large-scale models are of little use in policy analysis and evaluation.[14] What these critical studies have shown is that the path

12. For example, Edward R. Tufte, ed., *The Quantitative Analysis of Social
Problems*, (Reading, Mass.: Addison-Wesley, 1970) and David C. Hoaglin, Richard
J. Light, Bucknam McPeek, Frederick Mosteller, and Michael A. Stoto, *Data for
Decisions* (Cambridge, Mass.: Abt, 1982).

13. Ravetz, *Scientific Knowledge*, 122.

14. For a small sample of the literature, see D. B. Lee, Jr., "Requiem for

from model to conclusions is long, involved, and beset by difficulties of all kinds. Only rarely can models provide full answers to policy questions. What they *can* do, if developed and used with care, is provide evidence which, together with other sources of information, may be used in arguments supporting a certain conclusion or recommendation. A good model is merely one type of evidence among others, not the end of the argument, much less the ultimate authority.

But to be used as evidence, models must satisfy certain procedural requirements that make their assessment possible; they have to be "in proper form." It is not enough for an effective argument to have a particular form, such as the mathematical garb of an econometric model. After all, a mathematical style of presentation is not incompatible with a "black box" approach—it may even encourage it—and black-box models, it has been rightly said, "will never have an impact on policy other than through mystique, and this will be short-lived and self-defeating."[15]

A model is in proper form if the assumptions and the evidence used in it are presented in a sequence of steps that conform to basic rules of procedure analogous to those used when questions of law are debated in a court. This is far from being standard practice, as I pointed out in chapter 1. Hence, while it is important to insist, with the critics of large-scale policy models, that models be transparent and as simple as possible, it is also necessary to develop more detailed procedural guidelines, if models are to play their limited but potentially useful role in the policy process. It is indeed ironic that while data generation absorbs so much of the modeler's time and ingenuity, the transition from

Large-scale Models," *Journal of the American Institute of Planners* 39, no. 3 (1973): 163–78; W. Brian Arthur and Geoffrey McNicoll, "Large-scale Simulation Models in Population and Development: What Use to Planners?", *Population and Development Review* 1, no. 2 (Dec. 1975): 251–65; Garry D. Brewer, *Politicians, Bureaucrats, and the Consultant* (New York: Basic Books, 1973); B. A. Ackermann et al., *The Uncertain Search for Environmental Quality* (New York: Free Press, 1974); Martin Greenberger, Matthew A. Crenson, and Brian L. Crissey, *Models in the Policy Process* (New York: Russell Sage Foundation, 1976); and Martin Greenberger, *Caught Unawares* (Cambridge, Mass.: Ballinger, 1983).

15. Lee, "Requiem for Large-scale Models," 175.

data to conclusions should often rest on arguments that do not
bear close scrutiny. No amount of technical sophistication can
compensate for carelessness in structuring the arguments or in
drawing the necessary distinctions among data, information, evidence, and conclusions.

PITFALLS AND FALLACIES

The craft aspects of policy analysis are revealed most clearly by
the concept of *pitfall*. A pitfall is a conceptual error into which,
because of its specious plausibility, people frequently and easily
fall. It is the taking of a false logical path that may lead the
unwary to absurd conclusions. A pitfall is for the practical arguments used in policy analysis what the logical fallacy is in
deductive reasoning. In both cases, one has to be always on guard
against hidden mistakes that can completely destroy the validity
of a conclusion.

Logicians distinguish between a fallacy and a simple falsity.
A single statement may be false, but what is fallacious is the
transition from a set of premises to a conclusion. Similarly, in
policy analysis pitfalls should not be confused with blunders
or errors that may affect, for instance, the numerical value of
a solution but not the basic structure of the argument supporting it.

In logic there is a long tradition of systematic discussion of
fallacies that goes back to Aristotle. Nineteenth-century treatises
on logic always included one or more chapters on fallacies. John
Stuart Mill devoted Book V of *A System of Logic* to an account
and a new classification of fallacies, and A. DeMorgan, while
rejecting previous attempts to produce exhaustive descriptions
of all possible types of fallacy, nevertheless devoted an entire
chapter of his *Formal Logic* to a penetrating analysis of many of
the traditionally listed pitfalls.

W. Stanley Jevons, one of the fathers of neoclassical economics, is also the author of a delightful book on elementary logic
in which, following Aristotle, fallacies are divided into logical
fallacies (those which occur in the mere form of a statement and,

thus, could in principle be discovered without any knowledge of the subject matter with which the argument is concerned) and material fallacies (which, being connected with the subject of the argument, can only be detected by those acquainted with the subject).[16]

Among the material fallacies Jevons listed are the fallacy of accident (arguing from a general rule to a special case, where a certain accidental circumstance renders the rule inapplicable, or arguing from a special case to a special case), the irrelevant conclusion (*ignoratio elenchi*, or arguing to the wrong point), the *petitio principi* (begging the question), the fallacy of the consequent (*non sequitur*) and the false cause (*post hoc ergo propter hoc*, or the assertion that one thing is the cause of another simply because it precedes, or accompanies, it). More recent contributions, mainly devoted to a discussion of fallacies in everyday reasoning, are Robert H. Thouless's *How to Think Straight* and Susan Stebbing's *Thinking to Some Purpose*.[17]

Outside logic and philosophy, the amount of attention devoted to the topic of pitfalls varies considerably among different disciplines. Very few natural sciences have standard literature on the possible pitfalls of their characteristic patterns of argument. This is not surprising, since in the natural sciences it is usually possible to make practical tests of theoretical conclusions, while the existence of effective mechanisms of quality control ensures the rapid elimination of gross fallacies. Also, laboratory courses help the student develop an intuitive feeling for the possibility of pitfalls in the standard procedures by which he verifies theoretical results.[18]

On the other hand, the literature of statistics, a discipline specifically concerned with the logic of inductive reasoning and the weighing of evidence, contains many insightful discussions

16. *Elementary Lessons in Logic* (1870; reprint, London: Macmillan, 1934), Lessons XX and XXI.

17. Robert H. Thouless, *How to Think Straight* (New York: Simon and Schuster, 1947); Susan Stebbing, *Thinking to Some Purpose* (1939; reprint, Harmondsworth, England: Penguin, 1959).

18. Ravetz, *Scientific Knowledge*, 94–101; E. Bright Wilson, Jr., *An Introduction to Scientific Research* (New York: McGraw-Hill, 1952), passim.

of pitfalls, both at the technical level—perhaps exemplified at their best by the published discussions of the British Royal Statistical Society—and in textbooks and popular expositions.[19] To some extent, this tradition has been carried over into the neighboring field of econometrics, but it does not seem to have penetrated deeply into actual econometric practice.[20]

An excellent collection of economic pitfalls, which every young policy analyst should read, is E. J. Mishan's *Twenty-one Popular Economic Fallacies*.[21] But, generally speaking, the social science literature reveals only a marginal awareness of the conceptual significance of pitfalls; for instance, the only detailed discussion of the topic in the eight-volume *International Encyclopedia of the Social Sciences* is the perceptive article on statistical fallacies by I. J. Good. As a result of this general lack of concern for the ever-present danger of pitfalls, certain types of inference rather widely used in past social science research have only recently been recognized as fallacious.

A good example from the sociological literature is W. S. Robinson's discovery of the so-called ecological fallacy. The pitfall consists of using ecological correlations (that is, statistical correlations involving properties of groups of individuals) as substitutes for individual correlations in which the correlates are properties of individuals: for instance, per capita rates of cigarette smoking and death rates from lung cancer in a number of countries, or race composition and literacy rates in different sections of a country. Correlation coefficients calculated in this way from national or regional averages can be quite misleading, since replacing each country or region by average values eliminates the spread around the averages and thus gives a wrong

19. W. Allen Wallace and Harry V. Roberts, *Statistics: A New Approach* (Glencoe, Ill.: Free Press, 1956); David Freedman, Robert Pisani, and Roger Purves, *Statistics* (New York: W. W. Norton, 1978); Darrell Huff, *How to Lie with Statistics* (Harmondsworth, England: Penguin, 1961).

20. J. S. Cramer, *Empirical Econometrics* (Amsterdam: North-Holland, 1969); Erich W. Streissler, *Pitfalls in Econometric Forecasting* (London: Institute of Economic Affairs, 1970); Edward E. Leamer, "Let's Take the Con out of Econometrics," *American Economic Review* 75, no. 1 (March 1983): 31–43.

21. *Twenty-one Popular Economic Fallacies* (Harmondsworth, England: Penguin, 1971).

impression of tight clustering. Robinson has shown that individual and ecological correlations are in general different (they may even differ in sign) and that the values of ecological correlations strongly depend on the type of grouping used.[22] These conclusions cast strong doubts on the validity of a number of empirical studies conducted in the past.

Even the great French sociologist Emile Durkheim has fallen into this pitfall in his famous study of suicide. From data on percentages of literates and suicide rates for each province in nineteenth-century Italy, Durkheim takes averages over three clusters of provinces, obtaining a correlation close to 0.9. From this he concludes that "popular education and suicide are distributed exactly in the same way."[23] Actually, correlation calculated from averages for each individual province turns out to be equal to 0.6, and even this value probably exaggerates the strength of the relationship.[24]

PITFALLS OF ANALYSIS

As already noted, in the natural sciences detailed discussions of different kinds of pitfalls can, to a large extent, be dispensed with because of the stock of practical knowledge that scientists have accumulated from long and successful experience. In policy analysis, however, direct verification of conclusions is seldom possible, while professional mechanisms for controlling the quality of analyses are still in an embryonic stage—the approach is too new for a widely shared tradition of critical thought to have developed.

Also, policy analysts have different disciplinary backgrounds, while students acquiring specialized training in undergraduate and graduate programs of public policy are exposed to academic curricula that vary from school to school and represent tentative

22. W. S. Robinson, "Ecological Correlations and the Behavior of Individuals," *American Sociological Review* 15 (1950): 351–57.
23. Emile Durkheim, *Le Suicide* (Paris: Presses Universitaires de France, 1960), 165.
24. Freedman, Pisani, and Purves, *Statistics*, 141–43.

compromises among different intellectual traditions. Most of the technical tools that the budding analyst is now required to learn have been developed by other disciplines, and textbook treatments tend to emphasize only those aspects that appear to have immediate practical usefulness. But concepts and techniques removed from their disciplinary matrix tend to become stereotypes, and their limitations are not easily perceived by people interested only in immediate applications. Such are the roots of some common pitfalls of analysis that B. O. Koopman has labeled "linearitis" (the erroneous belief that everything is linear), "maximitis" (the belief that the only or main purpose of analysis is to maximize something), and "mechanitis" (blind faith in the power of the computer and other mechanical aids). For the same reasons, all the subtlety of statistical reasoning is often lost in ritualistic and almost meaningless applications of hypothesis testing and significance levels.

Hence, a systematic study of pitfalls should become an important part of the training of policy analysts and public managers. As the philosopher of science Jerry Ravetz writes: "A recognition and systematic use of the phenomenon of pitfalls might be very effective in the teaching of those simple but essential craft skills which are involved in scientific, scholarly, or administrative work. An exposition of standard techniques in terms of the pitfalls they are designed to circumvent, with examples, could go far to make them meaningful and obviously worth mastering."[25] In fact, a number of standard works in the early literature of systems and policy analysis include fairly extensive treatment of pitfalls, and some of these discussions have attained the status of minor classics of the discipline.[26] This tradition is continued in a book edited by myself and Edward S.

25. *Scientific Knowledge*, 100.

26. B. O. Koopman, "Fallacies in Operations Research," *Operations Research* 4, no. 4 (1956): 422–26; Herman Kahn and Igor Mann, *Ten Common Pitfalls* (Santa Monica, Calif.: Rand Corporation, RM–1937, 1957); Charles J. Hitch and Roland N. McKean, *The Economics of Defense in the Nuclear Age* (Cambridge: Harvard University Press, 1960); Edward S. Quade, "Pitfalls and Limitations," in E. S. Quade and W. I. Boucher, eds., *Systems Analysis and Policy Planning* (New York: American Elsevier, 1968), 345–63.

Quade, in which a number of experienced analysts survey the entire spectrum of possible pitfalls of analysis, from problem formulation to implementation.[27]

Here it is not possible to do more than to treat selectively some of the more common types of pitfalls. It will be convenient to organize the discussion under four headings that closely correspond to the four components of the analyst's work which have been identified above: data and information; tools and methods; evidence and argument; and conclusions.

Data and Information

Analysis usually begins with something less structured than a problem, namely, a problem situation. This is an awareness that things are not as they should be, but without a clear idea of how they might be corrected. Problem setting is the process of translating a problem situation into an actual policy problem stating the goals to be achieved and a strategy for accomplishing them.

The amount of detailed information that is useful at the stage of problem setting is different from what is needed when searching for solutions within a given formulation. The appropriate modes of inquiry will correspondingly differ in the two situations. Because of the unstructured character of a problem situation, imagination, judgment, and analogical and associative thinking play a bigger role in problem setting than rigor and technical skills.

Since the questions asked and the methodological decisions taken at this stage effectively condition the subsequent analysis, one must constantly be aware of the possibility of "preselecting" the final conclusions. For example, it may seem natural for an environmental agency working on a specific pollution problem to consider only alternatives falling in its jurisdiction. Even the competent analysts of the Delaware Estuary Comprehensive Study (DECS), discussed by Bruce Ackermann and his coauthors, chose to define their inquiry to the Delaware Estuary, for which

27. *Pitfalls of Analysis* (New York: Wiley, 1980).

they were directly responsible, instead of considering other, and probably better, alternatives for outdoor recreation.[28]

The next task facing the DECS analysts was to define the nature of the pollution problem in the Delaware River. Traditionally, the amount of dissolved oxygen (DO) in the water has served sanitary engineers as the principal indicator of water quality. It is therefore understandable that the DECS engineers would take recourse to the received wisdom of their profession. But this technical decision had major policy consequences. Once DO was accepted as the relevant indicator, the section of the river experiencing the most serious pollution problem and urgently requiring public action was automatically identified: it was the heavily industrialized region between Philadelphia and Wilmington suffering the most acute oxygen sag. Although there was no reason to believe that increasing DO to feasible levels in this critical section of the river would make the Delaware more suitable for recreational and other uses, this became in fact the focus of the technical analyses. And because the economists responsible for the cost-benefit part of the study accepted uncritically the engineers' formulation of the problem, the policy alternatives from which the agency had to choose came to be expressed in terms of different DO levels. Incidentally, this instructive example reveals another pitfall whose importance has not been sufficiently recognized in the literature. It is often said that any analyst who accepts the client's initial formulation of the problem uncritically is heading for a disaster. The case of the DECS shows that it is an equally serious mistake to accept uncritically the initial problem formulations of technical experts.

The production and interpretation of data present peculiar problems at the problem-setting stage of the analysis. Thus, information obtained through opinion polls or attitude surveys is particularly sensitive to the way the questions are framed, which in turn may depend on how the problem is conceived. The distinction between facts and artifacts, always a tricky one when social and economic data are involved, becomes particularly difficult when one tries to find out what the problem is. To say,

28. Ackermann et al., *The Uncertain Search for Environmental Quality.*

for example, that 7 percent of the labor force is unemployed is only to say that this is the result of applying certain operations embodied in a questionnaire and the answers to it. A simple change in one question, or in some definition, may produce a significant change in the number of unemployed.[29]

A related pitfall is the failure to recognize the large margin of error surrounding all socioeconomic statistics. National income statistics probably cannot be known with a smaller margin of error than ± 10 to 15 percent, and comparable uncertainties are present in foreign trade, price, unemployment, and growth statistics.[30] Hence, a reported drop of one or two percentage points in a country's gross national product may or may not be a significant indication that immediate government action is required. Similarly, serious biases in unemployment statistics (due, for example, to various work registration requirements for welfare recipients) have been identified by a number of government bodies and academic experts, but policymakers continue to base their decisions on the existing unreliable statistics.[31]

In fact, all social and economic indicators are the product of definition and convention. Measures of inflation, production, education, health, or crime must always be interpreted in relation to a specific context before they acquire any operational meaning; their usefulness depends entirely on a clear recognition of their conventional character. Hence, economic and social statistics cannot be treated in the same way we treat "facts" or physical measurements obtained from a direct apprehension of some natural phenomenon. In Allan Coddington's apt phrase, one cannot, even with good eyesight, go out into the Treasury steps and observe the domestic level of economic activity. Rather, "economic statistics are the result of the bureaucratic compounding

29. W. E. Deming, "Boundaries of Statistical Inference," in N. L. Johnson and H. Smith, Jr., eds., *New Developments in Survey Sampling* (New York: Wiley-Interscience, 1969), 656.

30. The classic reference here is Oskar Morgenstern, *On the Accuracy of Economic Observations*, 2d ed. (Princeton, N.J.: Princeton University Press, 1963).

31. Kenneth W. Clarkson and Roger E. Meiners, "Government Statistics as a Guide to Economic Policy: Food Stamps and the Spurious Increase in the Unemployment Rates," *Policy Review* 1, no. 1 (Summer 1977): 27–47.

of enormous quantities of fragmentary and even ambiguous pieces of information: the components are thrown up as a result (or even as a by-product) of the general administrative processes of society, from tax-returns, sample surveys, censuses, and so on; the components are assembled and aggregated by teams of statisticians who have not themselves collected the information. And the amount of information involved is vast. Presumably, we can learn more from imperfect statistics than from no statistics at all, provided that their conventional basis and degree of reliability are appreciated."[32]

The ad hoc nature of much social and economic accounting—the fact that the classificatory schemes used in data collection are more often dictated by expediency (the availability of data, the feasibility of certain estimates, the standard operating procedures of the data-gathering organization) than by logical or theoretical considerations—is seldom publicized by the data collectors and may be overlooked by the data users. Erich Streissler, a distinguished Austrian economist, tells the story of the econometrician who once made the rather surprising discovery that in Austria profits rose over a certain period exactly as much as wages and salaries. The econometrician had apparently forgotten that in the early days of Austrian national income accounting, profits were *assumed*—for lack of data—to move in proportion to wages and salaries![33]

Sometimes the analyst is in the fortunate position of being able to collect the primary data, or at least of suggesting an appropriate sampling design. Even then the original data are usually much too raw to be used in a model or in an analytic argument without first being refined into a more reliable and useful form. Such refining requires craft skills that are rather different from those used in problem setting and data collection.

The transformation of data into information involves three basic judgments, all of which present the risk of serious mistakes. The first concerns the possible loss of important details: since in most policy problems a "sufficient statistic," containing exactly

32. "Are Statistics Vital?", *The Listener* (11 Dec. 1969): 823.
33. Streissler, *Pitfalls*, 28.

the same amount of information as the original sample, does not exist, data reduction may involve too great a loss of information relative to the problem under discussion.

The second is a judgment of the goodness of fit of a model to the original data, a problem for which standard statistical techniques are available. The third basic judgment is that this particular transformation of the data, among the many possibilities, is the significant one.

An entertaining example of a pitfall involving the third kind of judgment is given by Quade: the use, during World War I, of the arithmetic instead of the harmonic mean in computing turnarounds of troop and cargo ships of different speeds.[34] This is, admittedly, a rather trivial mistake (though a frequent one, as tests in undergraduate statistics courses show), but precisely its elementary character shows how easy it is to stumble into pitfalls in even the simplest aggregation of data.

Tools and Methods

The tools of policy analysis may be roughly classified according to their function in conceptualization, in data production and manipulation, and in interpretation. The category of conceptual and interpretive tools includes disciplines such as mathematics, economics, and the political and behavioral sciences, which the analyst has to master to some extent in order to do competent work.

I have already alluded to the possibility of pitfalls arising when certain concepts or methods are taken out of their broader disciplinary context. For example, to noneconomists "cost" usually means historical or sunk cost, rather than opportunity cost. A number of early applications of operations research are vitiated precisely by this conceptual mistake. Similarly, "average" is often taken to mean arithmetic or sample average even when, as in the example of the harmonic mean just mentioned, another measure is more appropriate. Again, engineers, being accus-

34. E. S. Quade, *Analysis for Public Decisions*, 2d ed. (Amsterdam: North-Holland, 1982), 319–20.

tomed to operate with input-output ratios, tend to use ratios of benefits to costs as measures of efficiency, disregarding the absolute sizes of benefits and costs.

The danger of conceptual pitfalls is made particularly acute by the prevailing metaphysics, according to which the scientific character of a field is assumed to be in direct proportion to the degree of its mathematical formalization. As a result, the analyst is sometimes tempted to use formal tools that exceed the level of his mathematical or statistical sophistication, and whose range of meaningful applicability he is therefore incapable of assessing.

In disciplines with a long intellectual tradition the introduction of new tools usually opens up lines of research that were previously inaccessible. In newer fields of inquiry, on the other hand, we often witness the phenomenon of "new toolism," a disease to which policy analysts seem to be particularly predisposed. Those affected by this disease "come possessed of and by new tools (various forms of mathematical programming, vast air-battle simulation machine models, queuing models, and the like), and they look earnestly for a problem to which one of these tools might conceivable apply."[35]

In the preceding pages we have seen how difficult it is to obtain information that is both reliable and relevant. The difficulties are compounded when the data are processed by means of formal techniques and models. For example, are the results derived from a particular model more sensitive to changes in the model and in the methods used to estimate its parameters, or to changes in the data? No general answer to this question seems to be available, and the limited evidence is conflicting. Thus, one econometric study finds that the choice of estimation procedure has more effect on the parameter estimates than the choice of data, while another study concludes that the variations in parameter estimates are generally much greater between different sets of data than between different methods of estimation.[36]

35. Albert Wohlstetter, "Analysis and Design of Conflict Systems," in E. S. Quade, ed., *Analysis for Military Decisions* (Amsterdam: North-Holland, 1970), 106.

36. K. Holden, "The Effect of Revision of Data on Two Econometric

Regression methods are among the most popular tools of applied social research and policy analysis; yet it is often forgotten that the meaning of a fitted equation

$$y = b_0 + b_1 x_1 + b_2 x_2 + \ldots + b_r x_r$$

differs according to whether the x's represent planned or unplanned ("passive") observations. The same formal data manipulations are carried out in both cases, but in the case of passive observations (as in studies correlating income and educational levels, or industrial production and population) it would be quite misleading to interpret the coefficient b_i as measuring the effect on y of a unit change in x_i. Such an interpretation is justifiable only if the observations come from a planned experiment. As statistician George Box remarks, to find out what happens to a system when you interfere with it you have to interfere with it, not just passively observe it.[37]

Evidence and Argument

The argument is the link connecting data and information with the conclusions of the analysis. As already noted, the structure of the argument typically will be a complex blend of factual statements, interpretations, opinions, and evaluations. Hence, whatever testing is done must rely on a variety of professional standards, corresponding to the different theories and methods employed; on the plausibility of the results and their robustness with respect to variation in the underlying assumptions and specifications; and on the criteria of adequacy of the client, or the rules of argument prevailing in the relevant forum of debate.

The nature of the evidence plays a crucial role here, since a wrong assessment of its strength and fit before it is included in the argument can lead to pitfalls in the drawing of conclusions. Even a style of presentation that is inappropriate for the audi-

Studies," *The Manchester School of Economics and Social Studies*, March 1969, 23–37, quoted in Ravetz, *Scientific Knowledge*, p. 84; F. J. Denton and J. Kuiper, "The Effect of Measurement Errors on Parameter Estimates and Forecasts," *Review of Economic and Statistics* 47 (1965): 198–206.

37. "Use and Abuse of Regression," *Technometrics* 8, no. 4 (1966): 629.

ence to which the argument is directed can destroy the effectiveness of information as evidence.

Among the most widespread pitfalls related to evidence and arguments, three deserve special notice. The first originates in the contemporary fashion of using mathematical formalizations on every possible occasion. Two experienced analysts observe that "the analyst often dresses up his results and attempts, either consciously or unconsciously, to hide fairly elementary notions in extreme mathematical and technical language. Though it is probably not possible to condense the most esoteric results of modern mathematics and physics into the language of the newspapers, this is just not true of any applied operations analyses that we have seen."[38]

It should be added that an overly formalized style of presentation not only obscures the real issues and impedes assessment of the plausibility of the conclusions; it also induces a tendency to accept statistical information or the results of mathematical calculations as facts rather than evidence.

The second group of pitfalls is encountered when existing information is taken over for use in an analytic argument. All kinds of distortions occur when data gathered by one organization for broadly defined purposes are used by others to support specific conclusions. Whether such material is of sufficient strength and fit for its function in the argument depends on the mode of its original production; this is often difficult for the analyst to assess and usually impossible for him to change.

Finally, questions concerning the acceptable degree of approximation of numerical results or the acceptable level of precision of a set of data acquire their full meaning, for policy analysts at any rate, in connection with the use of evidence. Two other pitfalls should be mentioned in this context: the belief that there is an absolute standard of adequacy, and the rejection of items of information or opinions for which consensus among the experts is lacking. The belief in absolute standards overlooks the fact that even the physical sciences simultaneously use several degrees of acceptable levels of precision for their data. For ex-

38. Kahn and Mann, *Ten Common Pitfalls*, 47.

ample, some physical constants are known with an accuracy of 10^{-14}, while the age of the earth can only be estimated with an error of billions of years. Because of the diversity of the data used in a typical analytic study, the acceptable margins of error may have to be even larger than those the economist or the sociologist must realistically accept. This does not mean, of course, that the analyst should not have high standards of quality for his evidence; the pitfall consists in setting the standards so high that they become self-defeating.

Conclusions

The conclusion of a policy study may be a prediction, a recommendation, an evaluation of ongoing programs, a new proposal, or a different perspective on an old problem. Whatever its nature, a conclusion always depends on a number of assumptions and methodological choices. A different conceptualization of the problem, other tools and models, or a few different judgments made at crucial points of the argument could lead to quite different conclusions.

Thus, the contact with the external world of real people and their problems is always indirect and elusive. This is true of any kind of intellectual inquiry, including natural science. But in science the pitfalls encountered when a theory makes contact with reality can be detected, before too much harm is done, by various means—including controlled experiments and working models—that reduce the abruptness of the impact. In policy analysis such tests are seldom, if ever, available. How, then, can one control the validity of a conclusion, make sure that it is not fallacious?

To repeat, policy problems are not textbook quizzes; they carry no guarantee that there always exist correct solutions against which analytic conclusions may be checked. Unlike the analyses of military operations conducted during World War II, and some small-scale industrial and administrative applications, it is extremely difficult to evaluate the usefulness of large-scale policy studies in terms of actual results produced. This is due to a number of reasons: first, the long time lag between the adoption of a policy recommendation and its actual implementation; second, the difficulty of sorting out the effects of a particular decision from among a multitude of confounding factors; third, and most important, the fact that the political and institutional context in which policy studies are done, has changed considerably over the years. In the early days of operations research and systems analysis the relationship between decision maker and adviser, between producer and user of analysis, was clearer and more direct than it is today. Now it is quite common for policy research to be sponsored by one organization, carried out by another, utilized by a third organization, and perhaps evaluated by yet another agency (which, in turn, may entrust the evaluation to an independent research group). Clearly, the criteria of effectiveness of the sponsors are not the same as those of the users, or of the controllers. Thus, analysts must satisfy a number of different, sometimes conflicting, expectations. The best they can do is to achieve some acceptable level of adequacy along each dimension; they must "satisfice" rather than maximize any one particular criterion.

CRITERIA OF ADEQUACY

We have shown that the work of the analyst is guided and controlled by many informal judgments concerning the different aspects of the problem under investigation. The precepts of a craft can never be fully articulated, but despite the absence of explicit rules a connoisseur has little difficulty in distinguishing good from poor craftsmanship. This is because the true connoisseur has an intimate knowledge of what might be called the microstructure of the artist's style.

Similarly, in order to appreciate the craft aspects of analysis and to evaluate competently the quality of the finished product one must learn to examine the microstructure of arguments. This was the purpose of breaking down the analyst's task into its component elements. Such a detailed examination would have only academic interest if it were possible to assess the quality of a policy analysis simply by comparing its conclusion with policy outcomes. A single synthetic criterion would be sufficient in this case: the analysis is good if the policy succeeds, and bad otherwise.

But, as I have said, policy problems carry no guarantee that there exist correct solutions against which the analyst's conclusions could be checked. Policies usually fail in some respects and succeed in others, and the relationship between what the analyst does, or says, and the final outcome is always indirect and uncertain. One recurrent theme in the evaluation literature is the call to develop methods that emphasize outcome rather than process. Outcome-oriented evaluation has a strong intuitive appeal, but in the case of professional work the outcome/process dichotomy is not very useful. A well-known medical expert has stated that "much, perhaps most, of what a physician does must be categorized as process, and process not even calculated to affect outcome."[39] To a greater or lesser extent the same is true of all professionals, including policy professionals.

Hence process-oriented criteria of adequacy are necessary, although not sufficient, to assess the quality of analysis. A policy analysis is adequate if it meets the particular tests that are appropriate to the nature, context and characteristic pitfalls of the problem. Different criteria apply to the separate elements of the analysis, as exemplified in the following table:

Analytic component	Criteria of adequacy
Data	Reliability, reproducibility, credibility (for exogenous data)
Information	Relevance, sufficiency, goodness of fit, robustness
Evidence	Reliability, admissibility, strength
Argument	Cogency, persuasiveness, clarity
Conclusion	Plausibility, feasibility, acceptability

39. Walsh McDermott, "Evaluating the Physician and His Technology," in John W. Knowles, ed., *Doing Better and Feeling Worse* (New York: W. W. Norton, 1977), 138.

At the beginning of this chapter I asked how it is possible to define standards of quality, and thus avoid falling into methodological anarchism, once the claim to certainty of conclusions is abandoned. Process-oriented tests of adequacy are the answer, or at least part of the answer. Policy analysis can be neither performed competently nor used properly without an appreciation of its craft aspects.

Naturally, avoidance of pitfalls and other tests of adequacy only guarantee minimal standards of quality. They do not, and cannot, imply originality, depth, or any other of the intellectual qualities that distinguish the brilliant from the merely competent study. Nor do they guarantee that the analysis will be useful to the people who pay for it, or that it will have an impact on the public debate. The question of the utilization of knowledge in the policy process is considerably more complex and will be taken up in a subsequent chapter.

FOUR

Feasibility Arguments

To try to do something that is inherently impossible is, to borrow from Oakeshott, always a corrupting exercise. However, the tendency to equate the desirable with the feasible is always strong, especially in politics. As another philosopher has remarked, the existence of social tasks that appear both desirable and feasible but are in fact impracticable has set the stage for a wide range of conflicts in modern history. All the battles of social reform were fought partly on these grounds, with conservatives overstating and progressives underestimating the limit of the possible in public policy.[1]

Helping policymakers and public opinion avoid both harsh overstatement and reckless underestimation of those limits is one of the most useful contributions analysts can make to public deliberation. A competent feasibility analysis attempts to identify all actual or potential constraints, separate them from fictitious obstacles, evaluate their significance for different implementation strategies, and estimate the costs and benefits of relaxing those constraints that are not absolutely fixed.

1. Michael Polanyi, *The Logic of Liberty* (London: Routledge and Kegan Paul, 1951), 169.

Unfortunately, feasibility analysis is not always taken seriously. Policy analysts deal explicitly with a few easily quantifiable limitations, such as technical or budgetary constraints, but tend to treat political and institutional constraints, if at all, as second thoughts or last-minute caveats appended to an already hardened analytic structure.

It is a serious mistake to prescribe policy on the basis of such a narrow view of feasibility. There is no essential difference between technical, economic, political, institutional, or any other type of constraints: they all limit the freedom of choice of the policymaker, and their violation always entails a penalty. The fact that some constraints cannot be expressed in quantitative terms, like budget or other resource constraints, is irrelevant to the logic of the analysis. Even the "impossibility principles" of physics (such as the laws of conservation of energy and momentum) are not so much empirical laws or quantitative relations as expressions of a conviction that all attempts whatsoever to do a certain thing are bound to fail.

Occasionally such convictions have proved wrong (as in the case of the pre-Newtonian doctrine that a vacuum could not exist), but even then the attempt to show that repeated failures were due to something inherently impossible has been a source of new insights and discoveries. On the other hand, accepting too readily that something is impossible can impede progress, in public policy no less than in science and technology. Experience shows that with sufficient determination and imagination it is often possible to remove or relax many constraints, or to use them creatively to discover new possibilities.

The creative analyst must be able to maintain a dialectic tension between the practicable and the ideal—between probing the limits of public policy and trying to extend the boundaries of what is politically possible.

CONSTRAINTS AND IMPOSSIBILITIES

Before considering the political, economic and other constraints that are the main object of public debate and policy deliberation, it may be helpful to examine briefly how the notion of impossibility arises in more abstract contexts. Various kinds of impossibilities play a key role in mathematics and in science, and understanding that role will make it easier to appreciate the real significance of constraints in policy-making. Let us begin with elementary mathematics.

A number of classical problems of elementary algebra and geometry—squaring a circle, trisecting an arbitrarily given angle, or solving equations of degree five or higher, for example—involve "impossibility proofs." For centuries, outstanding mathematicians had tried in vain to find explicit solutions, until it was finally recognized that the crucial question was not: "By which method can such and such a problem be solved?", but rather: "How can one prove that certain problems have no solution?"

It is important to understand clearly the way this revolutionary question was formulated. With regard to the solution of equations, the problem was not to determine whether an algebraic equation of arbitrary degree could be solved. The existence of solutions had already been established by Gauss (in his doctoral dissertation of 1799), and a variety of numerical methods were available to calculate the roots to any desired degree of accuracy. The question that interested mathematicians like Ruffini and Abel in the first half of the nineteenth century was different and concerned the means—only rational operations and radicals—by which the solution was to be found.

Similarly, in order to decide which geometrical constructions are possible, it was first necessary to define precisely the meaning of *construction*, again by specifying the means—ruler and compass, for example—that are allowed in each case. As it turned out, such impossibility problems could not be resolved within the domain of elementary geometry and algebra, but required radically new concepts and profound theoretical developments, such as Galois' theory of groups.

This chapter in the history of mathematics has several interesting lessons for policy analysts. First, it shows that it is often more fruitful to ask what cannot be done and why, rather than what can be done. Faced by what appears to be an intractable policy problem, it is good strategy for the analyst to stop and think about possible reasons for the repeated failures before embarking on a search for new solutions.

Second, our mathematical examples remind us that no problem can be called solvable or unsolvable until it is clearly understood which methods of solution are admitted and which are excluded. A related point is that a problem may be solvable in a technically well-defined sense without being solvable under the additional constraints that must be considered when the technical solution is applied to a concrete historical situation. Thus, economic theory may indicate a way of obtaining an optimal stable price and employment system, but the solution depends on assumptions of perfect labor mobility and price flexibility that cannot be satisfied in practice. In practically any field of public policy one can find examples where optimal or satisfactory solutions are known to exist but cannot be implemented because they presuppose a level of knowledge and an institutional flexibility that are not to be found in the real world.

Finally, there are cases in public policy, as in mathematics, where a problem that has a known solution with a given set of means is made unsolvable (at least temporarily) by a sudden restriction of the means. For example, when a country joins a supranational organization like the European Community it can no longer use some of the traditional instruments of monetary, trade, and industrial policy, and as a consequence it often faces severe adjustment problems.

In sum, problems are not solvable or unsolvable in general, but only with respect to certain constraints or limiting conditions. Notice that the limitations may be procedural (in our mathematical examples, using only ruler and compass or only rational operations and radicals) as well as substantive.

Physical laws are well-known instances of substantive constraints. Consider how scientific knowledge is used in technology. Scientific theories do not tell engineers how to achieve particular goals. Rather, they show why seemingly reasonable goals are in fact infeasible: why, for example, it is impossible to construct engines that are 100 percent efficient, or to eliminate friction completely, or to generate an electric charge without producing another charge of the opposite sign.

All theories express some kind of regularity or invariance and thus impose limits on the range of observable phenomena. Reality, Einstein once observed, restricts the wealth of possibilities; science attempts to discover these restrictions. Out of the set of all conceivable planetary motions, Newton's laws allow only elliptical ones. Scientific laws "do not assert that something exists or is the case; they deny it. They insist on the nonexistence of certain things or states of affairs, proscribing or prohibiting, as it were, these things or states of affairs; they rule them out."[2]

Entire branches of physics are based on such prohibitions or "postulates of impotence," as they have been called, and some scientists believe that all physical science and perhaps all natural science will some day be derived from a small number of such postulates. But how are these very general principles derived? Sir Edmund Whittaker, the physicist who coined the expression, acknowledges that they are not empirical laws. "A postulate of impotence," he writes, "is not the direct result of an experiment, or of any finite number of experiments; it does not mention any measurement, or any numerical relation or analytical equation; it is the assertion of a conviction that all attempts to do a certain thing, however made, are bound to fail."[3]

A postulate of impotence, even if it is not derived from experiments, codifies a great deal of practical experience in which something has been attempted by many routes and all of them have resulted in failure. The postulate supposes that this failure is due to something inherently impossible and thus saves us from wasting time on impossibilities like perpetual motion machines.

In this respect, physical impossibilities are not very different from generalizations in the social sciences, such as the "law" of supply and demand or the three basic principles of organizational control formulated by Anthony Downs: that no one can fully control the behavior of a large organization; that the larger an organization becomes, the weaker is the control over its actions exercised by those at the top; and that the larger an or-

2. Karl R. Popper, *The Logic of Scientific Discovery*, rev. ed. (London: Hutchinson, 1968), 69.

3. *From Euclid to Eddington: A Study of Conceptions of the External World* (New York: Dover, 1958), 69.

ganization becomes, the poorer is the coordination among its actions.[4] The obviousness of these principles does not reduce their significance; and although, like the postulates of impotence in physics, they cannot be proved, to disregard them could have very serious consequences.

However, these consequences may not be as immediately apparent as in the case of physical impossibilities. For this reason it is often politically difficult to resist the temptation to disregard economic or institutional constraints. Rent control is a classic example. Although the objective of controlling rents is to protect the consumer from the skyrocketing increases in rents that accompany a housing shortage, the long-run effect is to make almost everyone worse off by discouraging the construction of rental apartments and the upkeep of the existing stock, while encouraging the abandonment of old housing units or their conversion into office space in order to escape controls. These consequences have been known for some time, yet a number of cities that had abandoned rent control during the 1950s began to reinstitute this measure with the inflation of the 1970s.

In utopian phases of policy-making, even technical constraints are sometimes disregarded, with catastrophic consequences. For example, in the years immediately following the Soviet Revolution engineers were removed from their positions for questioning the technical feasibility of political goals. These experts became known as "limiters," and we learn from Alexander Solzhenitsyn that one Nikolai Ivanovich Ladyzhensky was arrested for supporting "limitation theories" and for "blind faith in safety factors."[5]

Like physical reality, social reality restricts the wealth of the possible. Our environment is extremely rich in constraints, both natural and man-made, and many of our basic concepts make use of them in essential ways. In fact, a world free of constraints would be utterly chaotic and unpredictable. If we often fail to recognize the presence of constraints the reason is that we are so familiar with them that we take them for granted. But it is

4. *Inside Bureaucracy* (Boston: Little, Brown, 1966), 140–43.
5. *The Gulag Archipelago*, trans. M. Scammell (London: Collins, 1974), 45.

```
>SET TT17: WIDTH:132
>SET TT17: FORM
>;
>SET TT20: LOWER
>SET TT20: SPEED:9600
>SET TT20: MODEL:VT100
>SET TT20: WIDTH:132
>SET TT20: FORM
>;
>QUE /START:QMG
>;
>QUE AL00:/NM/CR:P
>QUE AL01:/NM/CR:P
>QUE AL02:/NM/CR:P
>QUE RL00:/NM/CR:P
>QUE RL01:/NM/CR:P
>QUE RL02:/NM/CR:P
>QUE LP00:/NM/CR:P
>QUE LP01:/NM/CR:P
>;
>INS LB:$LPP/TASK=TT5/PRI=100
>QUE TT5:/NM/CR:P
>QUE TT5:/SH/SP
>QUE TT5:/ASS:AL00
>QUE TT5:/ASS:AL01
>QUE TT5:/ASS:AL02
>INS LB:$LPP/TASK=TT7/PRI=100
>QUE TT7:/NM/CR:P
>QUE TT7:/SH/SP
>QUE TT7:/ASS:RL00
```

```
>SET TT21; WIDTH=132
>SET TT21; FORM

>SET TT20; LOWER
>SET TT20; SPEED:9600
>SET TT20; NOTE1:VT100
>SET TT20; WIDTH=
>SET TT20; FORM

>QUE /START:ONS

>QUE AL00:/NM/CR:P
>QUE AL01:/NM/CR:P
>QUE AL02:/NM/CR:P
>QUE RL00:/NM/CR:P
>QUE RL01:/NM/CR:P
>QUE RL02:/NM/CR:P
>QUE LP00:/NM/CR:P
>QUE LP01:/NM/CR:P

>INS LB:#LPP:/TASK=TT5/PRT=100
>QUE TT5:/NM/CR:P
>QUE TT5:/SH/SP
>QUE TT5:/ASS:AL00
>QUE TT5:/ASS:AL01
>QUE TT5:/ASS:AL02
>INS LB:#LPP/TASK=TT7/PRT=100
>QUE TT7:/NM/CR:P
>QUE TT7:/SH/SP
>QUE TT7:/ASS:RL00
```

sufficient to attempt to enumerate the obstacles that face us even in the most ordinary activities to realize that our environment is largely composed of constraints.

FEASIBILITY AND SECOND-BEST SOLUTIONS

Learning to appreciate the pervasiveness of constraints is a good antidote to a common tendency of lay persons and social scientists alike to see power everywhere and to explain policy outcomes exclusively as the result of the deliberate actions of powerful individuals and groups. In reality, policymakers are often less powerful than they are assumed to be. A particular outcome may be the unintended by-product of previous policies or the result of bureaucratic processes that in no way had that outcome "in mind." But even to understand the strength of a powerful policymaker one must begin by marking out the limits upon his specific powers.

The American presidency is certainly one of the most powerful institutions in the world. Yet, as Richard Neustadt writes, "the President's advantages are checked by the advantages of others. Continuing relationships will pull in both directions. These are relationships of mutual dependence. A President depends upon the men he would persuade; he has to reckon with his need or fear of them. They too will possess status, or authority, or both, else they would be of little use to him. Their vantage points confront his own; their power tempers his."[6] In assessing the power of any policymaker, many other limits must also be taken into consideration: prior policies and institutional inertia; inadequate, outdated, or wrong information; cognitive limitations; the plans of other policymakers and the resistance of one's own bureaucracy; vested interests and the demands and aspirations of different social groups; limits on the span of control and on the available time and resources; authority leakage and loss of legitimacy; foreign commitments and international pressures. While most of these limits will not be so tight as to

6. *Presidential Power* (New York: Wiley, 1963), 44.

allow the policymaker no leeway, they are of sufficient significance that ignoring them will cause serious and sometimes dis-
astrous consequences.

Hence, the analyst must be aware of facile analogies between
public policy-making and entrepreneurial decision making. For
example, proponents of an economic theory of democracy such
as Anthony Downs have argued that people in government
achieve their goals by adopting those programs which please
voters most, just as entrepreneurs make profits by producing
things people want.[7] This analogy is misleading to the extent
that it suggests more freedom of choice than is normally available
to public policymakers. Unlike the entrepreneur, the policymaker is not free to shift resources from one area to another,
except marginally. His freedom is limited by budgetary rules,
political bargains, and the growing portion of public revenues
that are automatically committed to the public debt, to salaries
and pensions, and to a fairly small number of high-priority items.
Even the possibility of substituting one input for another in order
to take advantage of new opportunities and particular circumstances is severely limited by the requirements of fiscal accountability. As Ludwig von Mises has repeatedly pointed out, the
freedom of public managers to adjust their acts to what seems
to them the most appropriate solution of a concrete problem is
limited by norms especially designed to limit a discretion which,
unlike the discretion of the private manager, is not restricted by
considerations of profit and loss.[8]

These pervasive limitations on the power of policymakers explain why optimization is such an elusive goal in the public sector
that suboptimal solutions will usually be the only feasible ones.
A formal proof of this fact is provided by the second-best theorem of welfare economics. Essentially, this theorem states that
the first-order conditions for an optimum are not, in general,
valid policy criteria in a situation where, because of some constraint added to the usual budgetary and technical limitations,

7. Anthony Downs, *An Economic Theory of Democracy* (New York: Harper and
Row), 1957.
8. *Human Action*, 3d ed. (Chicago: Regnery, 1966).

the conditions cannot all be simultaneously satisfied.[9] For example, it may be politically impossible for the government to enforce the marginal-cost pricing condition throughout the economy. Should it try to enforce the condition at least in the publicly-owned sector of the economy? The answer given by the theorem of the second-best is: not necessarily. To achieve a second-best solution—one that satisfies also the additional constraint—it may actually be necessary to violate even those conditions that could have been implemented. Thus, the common assumption that it is better to fulfill at least some of the optimality conditions rather than none—that is, to pursue a policy of piecemeal optimization—turns out to be false.

But if suboptimal or second-best solutions are the only feasible ones, then it follows that feasibility, rather than optimality, should be the main concern of policy analysts, and that they should be as preoccupied with political and institutional constraints as with technical and economic limitations.

Moreover, once the question of feasibility is recognized in all its complexity, even the traditional ranking of policy alternatives—optimal, efficient, and feasible, in decreasing order of desirability—loses much of its meaning. In order to recommend a particular optimal policy from the set of Pareto-efficient alternatives—those that cannot be modified to increase the utility of some members of the community without reducing the utility of the other members—the analyst must be given a well-defined social welfare function. If none is available, the best he or she can do (in a normative sense) is to calculate the Pareto-efficient set. But in the absence of a social welfare function it is not at all clear that an efficient alternative is necessarily superior to one that is only feasible. For example, the *transition* from a nonefficient to an efficient situation need not be efficient, since some members of the community will probably be damaged by it and compensation may be politically infeasible. On the other hand, the transition between two feasible, but not efficient, situations could very well be Pareto-efficient since it may improve every-

9. Richard G. Lipsey and Kelvin Lancaster, "The General Theory of Second Best," *Review of Economic Studies* 24 (1956–1957): 481–92.

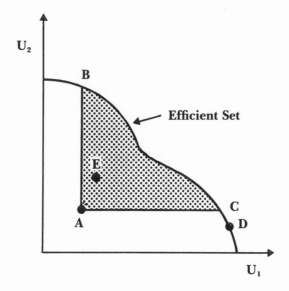

Fig. 1. Efficient and feasible policy alternatives in a community consisting of two individuals

one's position. Both cases are illustrated in figure 1, where we assume a community consisting of two individuals with utilities U_1 and U_2.

If A is the initial (feasible but not efficient) position and only Pareto-efficient moves are politically possible, the feasible alternatives are those in the shaded area, including the portion of the boundary (efficient set) between B and C. The first case is represented by a move from A to D. D is an efficient position (and hence "superior" to A), but the transition from A to D decreases U_2 and thus is not efficient. The move from A to E exemplifies the second case, in which there is an improvement even though both positions are "only" feasible.

POLITICAL FEASIBILITY

What do we mean when we say that only certain alternatives, like those represented by the shaded area in figure 1, are "politically" feasible? The notion of political feasibility is controversial. Some economists find it so flexible as to be almost useless as an analytic tool. Others argue that it should not even be considered in analysis. For example, Milton Friedman writes: "The role of the economist in discussion of public policy seems to me to be to prescribe what should be done in the light of what can be done, politics aside, and not to predict what is 'politically feasible' and then to recommend it."[10] On the other hand, James Buchanan, writing from the more pragmatic perspective of the student of public finance, observes that "to shy away from consideration of the politically feasible has been deemed an admirable trait; but to refuse to examine the politically possible is incomplete scholarship."[11] In fact, it is hard to see how Friedman's statement can be reconciled with the view (which seems to be accepted by a majority of economists today) that the effects of economic policy on efficiency cannot be separated from the effects on income distribution. For the problem is precisely that compensation payments are seldom feasible politically in a market economy, and hence all policy decisions must be based on considerations of both efficiency and equity.

Actually, why should political obstacles to the implementation of an "economically correct" (or first-best) policy be placed outside the pale of normative analysis, when many of those obstacles arise out of the same rational behavior, the same assumptions of self-interest, that are taken for granted in the market? Of course, Friedman may only be suggesting that the economist, qua economist, is not competent to pass judgment on what is politically feasible and that he should restrict his pronouncements to questions of economic feasibility. With this one can only agree; but then, how is it possible to prescribe a policy on the basis of such narrow considerations? To prescribe "what should be done in the light of what can be done, politics aside" makes

10. "Comments on Monetary Policy," in *Essays in Positive Economics* (Chicago: University of Chicago Press, 1953), 264.

11. "Politics, Policy, and the Pigovian Margins," in J. M. Buchanan and R. D. Tollison, eds., *Theory of Public Choice* (Ann Arbor: University of Michigan Press, 1972), 182.

sense only in a world in which politics and economics can be neatly separated, and where piecemeal optimization is possible.

This is certainly not the world in which policymakers live. If the purpose of analysis is not to *know* what is the correct policy in a given field but to *ensure* that the policy will be chosen and implemented, then it is essential to determine the limits within which the policymaker in question can exercise effective control.[12] Which policy instruments can be used? With whom does the policymaker need to share authority? Who are the political and bureaucratic actors whose support is needed? To answer such questions is to make certain assumptions about the political and institutional environment: behind every policy recommendation there is always a more or less implicit theory of government. Disregarding problems of political feasibility does not imply political neutrality, but rather the assumption that policy can be implemented by fiat. Knut Wickesell, a distinguished Swedish economist who wrote near the turn of the last century, had this naive theory of government in mind when he remarked that most economists are content with assuming perfect institutional plasticity and the rule of a benevolent dictator. Even the most recent manuals of public finance, he wrote, leave the impression "of some sort of philosophy of enlightened and benevolent despotism, and . . . seem to represent a running commentary on the famous rule 'Everything for the people, nothing by the people.' "[13] The same observation could be made about some of the most recent textbooks of policy analysis!

A more sophisticated understanding of the influences that affect government actions in a democracy is needed in order to deal adequately with questions of political feasibility. The following chapters will provide several examples of interactions between government activities and the political and institutional

12. A. K. Sen, "Feasibility Constraints: Foreign Exchange and Shadow Wages," in Richard Layer, ed., *Cost-Benefit Analysis* (Harmondsworth, England: Penguin, 1974), 140–59.

13. "New Principles of Just Taxation," in Richard A. Musgrave and Alan T. Peacock, eds., *Classics in the Theory of Public Finance* (London: Macmillan, 1967), 82.

environment. Here it is sufficient to raise the general question of how the notion of political feasibility can be made operational. By definition, a policy is feasible or infeasible only with respect to some specific constraints. Hence, in the case of political feasibility the analyst must be able to identify and evaluate the specific political constraints—institutional, bureaucratic, distributional, or political resource limitations—that restrict the freedom of choice of the policymaker in a particular situation.

Unless specific constraints can be identified, the concept of political feasibility is really too elastic to serve as a tool of analysis. For example, a policy is sometimes judged to be politically infeasible on the grounds that its political costs are too high. But the evaluation of the benefits and costs (political or otherwise) of a course of action is logically distinct from a judgment of feasibility. Presumably, a policymaker will not choose an alternative whose net benefit, taking all costs into consideration, turns out to be negative. This fact does not make the alternative infeasible, however, unless what is really meant is that the total resources required exceed some political "budget constraint." But then it would be much better to express the constraint directly in these terms, since this would force the analyst to estimate the nature and amount of the available political resources.

A TAXONOMY OF CONSTRAINTS

The identification of political and other constraints presupposes some classificatory scheme. However, constraints are so pervasive that they do not fall into a few simply described classes. Any classification, even one devised for a particular field of application, can be reasonably inclusive only by remaining at a high level of abstraction. Moreover, classifications are like methodological rules—always arbitrary to some extent, and arguable only with a particular purpose in mind. One important reason for classifying is simply to reduce the risk of overlooking some important constraint by means of a convenient checklist. The nature of the checklist naturally depends on the field of application.

For business applications, for example, the following classification has been suggested:[14]

a. market constraints
b. product constraints
c. technological constraints
d. organizational constraints
e. resource constraints

A somewhat different taxonomy would be appropriate for the cost-benefit analysis of a public project. A classification provided by Otto Eckstein for this purpose includes legal and distributional constraints in addition to the technological, resource, and administrative constraints in the above list.[15] It would be easy to lengthen the list by adding political, institutional, ethical, cognitive, and other kinds of constraints. But this way of proceeding would not be particularly useful in the present context since we are not discussing specific problems or techniques of analysis. Instead, it seems preferable to consider general taxonomic criteria which may then be used to derive more detailed and problem-specific classifications. The three criteria considered here correspond to basic distinctions between objective and self-imposed constraints, between goals and constraints, and between long-run and short-run limitations.

Objective versus Self-Imposed Constraints

This is probably the most important distinction for policy analysis. Obvious examples of objective constraints are physical and technological limitations, but there are many others. Just as physical laws reflect objective features of our natural environment, so the laws of the state, as Frederick Hayek pointed out, provide fixed features in our social environment. Hence, from the point

14. Samuel Eilon, "Prescription and Management Decision," *Journal of Management Studies* 6, no. 2 (1969), quoted in D. J. White, *Decision Methodology* (New York: Wiley-Interscience, 1975), 28.

15. "A Survey of the Theory of Public Expenditures," in James M. Buchanan, ed., *Public Finances: Needs, Sources, and Utilization* (Princeton, N.J.: Princeton University Press, 1961).

of view of a particular policymaker or actor, legal constraints are also objective despite the fact that they are man-made and not inviolable like natural or technical laws.

Budgetary and other resource limitations (such as political support, knowledge, technical know-how, information-processing capabilities, and time) are additional examples of objective constraints. Notice, however, that many resource constraints can be relaxed in the long run (see below), and the same is true of organizational and institutional constraints.

Objective constraints do not depend on our goals or values. We do not choose them; they are imposed on us. But many of the most important limitations on policy-making are not externally imposed; they are self-imposed, the result of a free choice or commitment. Once they are made, however, these commitments restrict the range of available alternatives in precisely the same way as do physical, technical, and other objective constraints. For example, the power to bind oneself is one of the most important tactics in bargaining. The negotiator who makes an irrevocable commitment to a certain course of action, and who succeeds in communicating it persuasively to the other party, has changed voluntarily and irreversibly the objective situation in which the negotiation takes place.[16]

This is only one example from the large class of self-imposed constraints. Heuristic constraints—the various assumptions, conventions, and methodological choices made in order to structure and simplify a problem and thus facilitate its solution—are another, very different example. Preselection, physicist Gerald Holton has observed, is the most significant element in moving from problem to solution. "There are many constraints," he writes, "which have been placed from the very beginning on the possible solution in an almost imperceptible manner; constraints on the 'facts,' on the hypothesis, on the correspondence between analogon and facts by which we are relieved of the feeling of puzzlement, by which we 'understand.' "[17] The author is dis-

16. Thomas C. Schelling, *The Strategy of Conflict* (New York: Oxford University Press, 1963).
17. *Thematic Origins of Scientific Thought* (Cambridge: Harvard University Press, 1973), 92.

cussing Plato's formulation of the problem of planetary motion, but his observation applies to any kind of problems, including policy problems.

As these examples suggest, the variety of self-imposed constraints is quite large. For practical purposes such constraints may be categorized as follows:

   a. Constraints that are adopted for a limited purpose or time (for example, heuristic constraints, contractual commitments, promises, conventional definitions or interpretations of certain terms in a document).

   b. Constraints that are accepted "until further notice" because they are considered important or useful (for example, strategic commitments by which one binds oneself in continuous negotiations, administrative procedures and routines, classificatory schemes).

   c. Constraints that are considered to be indispensable for the achievement of certain policy goals (for example, distributional constraints, rules of reciprocity, "due process," consistency, precedents, deference to other policymakers).

   d. Constraints that are accepted implicitly, but whose existence is acknowledged only when they are challenged or violated (for example, cultural norms, rules of etiquette, professional standards, tacit agreements, preselection in problem formulation).

Goals versus Constraints

In a sense, goals are self-imposed limitations. In choosing a goal one commits oneself to a certain range of activities, thereby eliminating many other possibilities. On what basis, then, do we differentiate goals from constraints? Consider a policymaker who feels that a particular concern is so important that it should be treated as a binding constraint. Wouldn't his ends be better served by including that concern in his objective function? Why use self-imposed constraints rather than goals to be maximized subject only to objective limitations? Economic policy aimed at improving allocative efficiency should also satisfy requirements for a more equitable distribution of income. What difference does it make, if any, whether these distributional concerns are expressed as constraints or are incorporated into the objective function?

A mathematically sophisticated analyst may be inclined to deny that a real problem exists here. After all, a constrained optimization problem can be transformed, with some ingenuity, into a problem (or sequence of problems) in which the constraints have been moved into the objective function. One well-known method for doing this is through Lagrange multipliers, and other methods based on the use of "penalty functions" adjoined to the original objective have been developed.[18]

Also, a distinguished organization theorist doubts that there is a meaningful distinction between goals and constraints. Herbert Simon writes:

> It is doubtful whether decisions are generally directed toward a goal. It is easier and clearer to view decisions as being concerned with discovering courses of action that satisfy a whole set of constraints. It is this set, and not any one of its members, that is most accurately viewed as the goal of the action. If we select any of the constraints for special attention, it is (a) because of its relation to the motivations of the decision maker or (b) because of its relation to the search process that is generating or designing particular courses of action. Those constraints that motivate the decision maker and those that guide his search for actions are sometimes regarded as more "goal-like" than those that limit the actions he may consider, or those that are used to test whether a potential course of action he has designed is satisfactory. Whether we treat all the constraints symmetrically or refer to some asymmetrically as goals, is largely a matter of linguistic or analytic convenience.[19]

Simon is right in stressing that decision makers are mainly concerned not with optimizing but with discovering feasible courses of action, but does it follow that the choice between placing a value in the goal or in the constraint set is only a matter of linguistic or analytic convenience? A moment's reflection

18. See, for example, A Fiacco and G. McCormick, *Nonlinear Programming: Sequential Unconstrained Minimization Techniques* (New York: Wiley, 1968).

19. "On the Concept of Organizational Goal," *Administrative Science Quarterly* 9, no. 1 (1964): 20.

shows that, in fact, the issue involves a genuine choice between two approaches with quite distinct implications.

In the terminology of Robert Nozick, treating the value as an argument in the decision maker's objective function corresponds to an end-state maximizing (utilitarian) view, while the alternative approach reflects a side-constraints (Kantian) view.[20] Values incorporated in an objective function can always be traded off at the margin. A good utilitarian is prepared to sacrifice some of any goal to obtain more of other goals. Within a maximizing structure a goal may (indeed, should) be sacrificed if this leads to an improvement in the level of total utility. However, a constraint cannot be traded off against other constraints or goals. This is clear in the case of objective constraints that are completely outside our control. But even self-imposed constraints lose their meaning and practical usefulness if they can be exchanged and redefined at will. Thus, the choice between goals and constraints is more than a matter of mere convenience. The criterion for deciding whether a value should be treated as a policy goal or a constraint is, in principle, straightforward: if the policymaker is willing to exchange that particular value (at the margin) against other values, then it should be treated as a goal; otherwise, as a constraint.

Short-run versus Long-run Constraints

Finally, any classification of constraints must pay attention to the time dimension. In the short run, technology, institutions, administrative capabilities, financial resources, and, in the very short run, even physical inputs and manpower must be taken as given. In a sufficiently long run these constraints can be relaxed, at a cost. The question whether a certain factor represents a binding constraint or just a "problem" can often be settled simply by distinguishing between the short and long run—provided one keeps in mind that the distinction does not refer to periods of calendar time, but to the time necessary to adapt fully to new

20. *Anarchy, State and Utopia* (Oxford: Blackwell, 1974).

conditions. Given sufficient time, technological limitations and institutional obstacles can be removed, laws changed, capacities increased, and new skills learned.

But while the range of feasible policies thus appears to be expanding, new constraints make themselves felt. These new constraints can arise in at least three different ways. First, the initial conditions of a policy problem are likely to change over time. As a consequence, the nature of the problem changes and new constraints arise. For example, the unemployment problem of today is certainly different from what it was in the 1960s, when the statistical evidence summarized in the "Phillips curve" seemed to prove the existence of a trade-off between unemployment and inflation. Recent experience has shown that high levels of inflation can coexist with high levels of unemployment and that, in fact, inflation can destroy jobs by undermining the incentive to spend and to invest. Accordingly, economists have worked out a new theory which maintains that the Phillips curve represents a valid short run constraint; in the long run, however, other constraints take over.

Implementation is a second, and very important, source of new constraints. At the time a policy is chosen it is impossible to know all the relevant limiting factors, and it is often difficult even to tell beforehand which of the assumed constraints will actually be binding. As the policy moves from decision to implementation, previously hidden constraints will emerge, forcing more or less radical policy changes. This iterative process of discovering constraints and modifying goals or strategies accordingly is the essence of policy implementation.

Third, factors that might be disregarded in the short run can become binding constraints in a long-run perspective. Thus, the need to maintain continuing cooperative relationships among policy actors imposes restrictions on acceptable behavior that can be ignored when agreement is needed only on a single issue. Again, low investments in research may not be a serious obstacle for a country in the early stages of economic development, but they become an increasingly important limitation as the economy matures. Many other examples easily come to mind.

In addition to the three basic distinctions just discussed—
between objective and self-imposed constraints, between goals
and constraints, and between short-run and long-run limitations—another, more technical distinction may be mentioned.
This is the distinction between deterministic and probabilistic
constraints. For example, it may be too difficult or too costly to
maintain a particular policy constraint under all conceivable circumstances, in which case one might like it to operate "most of
the time," allowing the constraint to be violated with a small
preassigned probability. Such "chance constraints," as they have
been called, are used mostly in business problems[21] but find
application also in public policy problems. Thus, environmental
standards defined by means of chance constraints allow analysts
to take into account extreme weather conditions, high waste
flows, fuel shortages, and other exceptional conditions when the
standards may be violated with a frequency not exceeding a
certain level.

In a more basic sense, most constraints of interest to policy
analysts are probabilistic since they are known only imperfectly.
In theory, this uncertainty could be expressed by the probability
distribution of the values that the constraint can assume. In
practice, data limitations usually force analysts to follow more
empirical approaches. They can perform sensitivity analyses to
study the effect of different constraint violations, attempt to
design more robust alternatives, recommend a cautious experimental strategy in the hope of finding out more about feasibility
conditions, or even suggest postponing a decision if the uncertainty is too great.

The taxonomic criteria we have discussed provide the skeleton
of a classificatory scheme around which a well-organized feasibility argument may be structured. But practically useful classifications tend to be problem-specific, and hence analysts must
decide in each case the level of detail that is appropriate for their
particular problem.

21. Abraham Charnes and William W. Cooper, *Management Models and Industrial Applications* (New York: Wiley, 1961).

CONSTRAINTS AND PSEUDO-CONSTRAINTS

A good classificatory scheme or checklist of constraints is an important first step in conducting a feasibility study. The crucial and more difficult task, however, is differentiating between real constraints and fictitious obstacles or pseudo-constraints set by mental or institutional inertia, risk aversion, lack of imagination or determination—or put up as an ideological screen to protect vested interests.

It is a mistake to think that genuine and false constraints can be distinguished on the basis of some special features present in one case and absent in the other. In an interesting essay on alleged constraints to economic development, Albert Hirschman argues that "the concept is far from solid, that it is not possible to identify either a finite number of 'reliable' obstacles to development or a hierarchy among these obstacles which would permit us to arrange them neatly into boxes marked 'basic,' 'important,' 'secondary,' et cetera."[22] He discusses three cases: alleged constraints that turn into assets ("blessings in disguise"); alleged constraints whose elimination turns out to be unnecessary; and constraints whose elimination is postponable. My intention here is not to discuss the substantive conclusions of Hirschman's argument, which concern the theory of economic development, but to question some of its broader methodological implications.

For example, Hirschman exposes the conceptual weakness of a method that consists of noting that some factors were present in the development of economically advanced countries, and then construing the absence of these same factors as constraints to development elsewhere. But the argument that certain alleged constraints turn out not to be binding in particular cases is not sufficient to support the conclusion that in such cases the notion of constraint is useless. Whether or not a constraint is actually binding in a given problem can often be determined only after

22. "Obstacles to Development: A Classification and a Quasi-Vanishing Act," in *A Bias for Hope* (New Haven: Yale University Press, 1971), 312.

the problem has been solved. Discovering redundancies in the constraint set can be an important part of the solution in many policy problems. Even when there are a priori reasons to believe that the constraint will not be binding, it may not be wise to ignore it, for it could become binding if some of the data and parameters of the problem change, perhaps as a result of new or better information. Both situations are well known in a number of different contexts, for example, in economic applications of linear programming methods.

Similarly, the fact that some constraints turn out to be "blessings in disguise" is less paradoxical than may appear at first sight, and certainly it does not prove that such blessings in disguise cannot be, at the same time, genuine constraints. In fact, once a constraint has been identified it is often possible to take advantage of it. The familiar phenomenon of friction is a good illustration. To technologists friction represents a pervasive and costly limitation, since it is impossible to build machinery that is completely free from it. A significant portion of the power used in running machinery (about 20 percent for a modern automobile) is wasted in overcoming friction. At the same time, friction is highly desirable in certain circumstances. Without it the wheels of a car would skid instead of going around; we could not walk with ordinary shoes, but would need suction pads to cling to the floor; knots would be ineffective since it is friction between the interlocking parts of the knot that holds it together; and a nail hammered into a piece of wood would be immediately squeezed out like a pip between our fingers.[23]

In sum, what distinguishes real from pseudo-constraints or fictitious obstacles is less their nature or particular characteristics than the quality of the supporting evidence. When an analyst asserts that something is technically or economically impossible, politically infeasible, or legally inadmissible, he is making an implicit commitment to produce arguments and evidence. In essence, the analyst is saying: G being what it is, you must rule

23. For a delightful discussion of the nuisance and desirability of friction, see Frank Philip Bowen and David Tabor, *Friction* (Garden City, N.J.: Anchor, 1973).

out A; to do otherwise would be V, and would invite P.[24] Here G stands for the grounds or reasons for asserting the constraint: a physical law, inadequate resources, institutional, legal, or logical impossibilities, implementation problems, and so on. A represents the alternative, or set of alternatives, ruled out by the constraint. The violation involved (V) and the possible penalty (P) will differ from case to case. Attempts to violate a physical or technical law are bound to end in failure; moving toward full employment at all costs will probably increase the level of inflation, and may cause a net loss of jobs in the long run; providing free health care will generate excess demand, long waiting lists, and a possible deterioration in the quality of the services; violating a legal norm will have serious penal consequences, while disregarding legitimate interests will make implementation more difficult and reduce the likelihood of reaching agreement on other issues in the future.

Thus, the same pattern of argument applies to such substantively different constraints as physical or logical impossibilities, economic limitations, legal prohibitions, and political infeasibilities. This is as it should be, since all constraints have a common logical form—expressed by terms such as: "cannot," "impossible," or the like—and the same practical implications: they all exclude some otherwise possible courses of action.

However, the grounds for accepting a constraint and the consequences of violating it vary in accordance with its nature. This becomes particularly clear when we contrast objective and self-imposed limitations. Many self-imposed constraints are introduced on utilitarian grounds. Hence, knowledge of their "opportunity cost" (that is, of the consequences for goal achievement of the resulting restriction in the range of feasible alternatives) is essential for a rational decision whether or not to accept them.

For example, the authors of a standard text of systems analysis write that "casually selected or arbitrary constraints can easily increase system cost or degrade system performance many-fold, and lead to solutions that would be unacceptable to the person

24. Stephen Toulmin, *The Uses of Argument* (Cambridge: Cambridge University Press, 1959), 30–35.

who set the constraints in the first instance if he understood their implications."[25] They cite the example of a weapon system study in which a constraint on acceptable casualties led to solutions in which $100 million was being spent, at the margin, to save a single life. Probably many more lives could have been saved by using the same resources in different ways; had the analysts realized the opportunity cost of these safety requirements, they might have considered other alternatives. But clearly such considerations are irrelevant in the case of physical and technical impossibilities, or any other objective constraints.

THE USES OF CONSTRAINT

I have emphasized the fact that all constraints, whether objective or self-imposed, natural or man-made, restrict our freedom of choice by eliminating certain courses of action. But it is equally important to keep in mind that constraints are, at the same time, essential conditions of rational behavior, and that they can be used to discover new possibilities.

A world free of constraints would be utterly chaotic and unpredictable; prediction is possible only in an environment structured by constraints. For example, serious technological forecasting differs from science fiction in that the forecasters discipline and control their conjectures by the systematic use of constraints and "principles of impotence" derived from the basic laws of nature.[26]

Learning, too, depends on the recognition and skillful exploitation of constraints. All organisms can learn and adapt only to the extent that their environment is constrained. In this respect the laws of the state are entirely analogous to the laws of nature. As Frederick Hayek points out, the effects of legal norms on the actions of an individual are "of precisely the same kind as those of the laws of nature: his knowledge of either enables

25. Charles Hitch and Roland N. McKean, *The Economics of Defense in the Nuclear Age* (New York: Atheneum, 1967), 186–187.

26. George Thomson, *The Forseeable Future* (Cambridge: Cambridge University Press, 1957).

him to foresee what will be the consequence of his actions, and it helps him to make plans with confidence.... Like the laws of nature, the laws of the state provide fixed features in the environment in which he has to move; though they eliminate certain choices open to him, they do not as a rule limit the choice to some specific action that somebody else wants him to take."[27]

In addition to searching for solutions within given constraints, the job of the analyst or policy adviser is to help push out the boundaries of the possible in public policy. Doing this requires both factual information and persuasion: what is politically feasible within given constraints, and even the constraints themselves, depend on the limits of popular knowledge and the relation of popularly accepted values to permissible practice. Hence, political constraints on policy can be eased only after public opinion has been conditioned to accept new thinking, new symbols, and new and broader concepts of the public interest.[28]

Keynes's contribution to the public debate on the problem of wartime finance in the late 1930s is an excellent example of this dual approach. From the outset, a recent biographer writes, "Keynes involved himself in the problems of war finance on two fronts—maximizing the possible under the existing constraints and easing the constraints themselves."[29] His arguments created a climate of opinion that made war and cheap money seem compatible to the authorities.

In order to get across the reasoning behind his plan and to find ways of making it more generally acceptable, Keynes engaged in a massive effort of education and persuasion. In addition to producing a stream of memoranda, articles, broadcasts, and letters to the press, he held numerous meetings with officials, politicians, academics, students, and trade union leaders. As a result of these discussions, he introduced several modifications into his original scheme of compulsory savings, such as family allowances to protect the low-paid with large families, stabiliza-

27. *The Constitution of Liberty* (London: Routledge and Kegan Paul, 1960), 153.

28. Walter W. Heller, *New Dimensions of Political Economy* (New York: W. W. Norton, 1967), 27.

29. D. E. Moggridge, *Keynes* (London: Macmillan, 1976), 116.

tion of the prices of the basic items of consumption, and a post-war capital levy to repay the compulsory savings and redistribute wealth. Thus, modified in a process of debate and mutual persuasion, Keynes's proposals gained wide acceptance and became the basis of wartime financial policy in Great Britain.

The role and influence of Keynes are probably unique in the annals of modern economic policy, but as a former chairman of the U.S. Council of Economic Advisers put it, all good policy advisers devote their time and energy not only to developing what is economically workable but to extending the boundaries of what is politically feasible.[30] Indeed, Max Weber reminds us that throughout history "man would not have attained the possible unless time and again he had reached out for the impossible."[31] Hence, creative policy-making requires both cool analysis and persuasion, or, to use Weber's words, both passion and perspective.

30. Heller, *New Dimensions of Political Economy*, 27.

31. "Politics as a Vocation," in H. H. Gerth and C. Wright Mills, eds., *From Max Weber* (New York: Oxford University Press, 1946), 128.

FIVE

Changing Institutional Constraints

Prominent among the man-made constraints discussed in the preceding chapter are institutions—laws, regulations, norms, organizations, decision-making procedures. The entire machinery of government, when viewed from this perspective, is a vast collection of constraints that define the roles of different policy actors and limit the range of strategies open to them. In the very short run, politicians, bureaucrats, interest groups, and private citizens must act within the rules defined by the existing institutional framework. In the longer run, however, the rules of the policy game can and do change. Policy actors not only pursue their goals within the limits set by the existing framework; they also strive to change those limits in their favor.

The possibilities open to policy actors of changing feasibility conditions through institutional change have not been always recognized. In welfare economics, for example, only the central policymaker (or benevolent dictator) is allowed to manipulate the constraints within which individuals and groups pursue their goals. This assumption is practically equivalent to asserting that no bridge exists between the behavior of people within given rules and their behavior as actors in the political process that defines and redefines the rules.

The model of institutional change presented in this chapter closes this gap by recognizing explicitly that policy actors are not artificially separated from the process that sets constraints on their behavior. The same people pursue their goals within the given institutional framework and attempt to modify that framework in their favor. In Victor Goldberg's apt phrase, the rules of the policy game both define the existing environment for choice and provide an arena for conflict.[1]

The implications of this extension of the traditional model of rational choice, in which institutions are taken as a constant for the purpose of policy analysis, are far-reaching. As we shall see in this and the next chapter, features of the policy-making process which appear contradictory when viewed from the traditional perspective can be explained quite naturally in terms of institution-changing behavior; strategies and policy instruments which seem superior when judged by criteria relevant to the traditional approach lose much of their attractiveness in the extended model.

THE ADVANTAGES OF ROUNDABOUTNESS

Eugen von Böhm-Bawerk, Austrian economist and statesman, based his famous theory of capital on the insight that roundabout methods of production are generally more efficient than direct methods—more fish can be caught by investing some time in constructing a net than by using one's bare hands. "That roundabout methods lead to greater results than direct methods," Boehm-Bawerk wrote, "is one of the most important and fundamental propositions in the whole theory of production."[2]

Institution-changing strategies are the policy equivalent of roundabout methods of production. Despite the substantial cost of modifying institutional constraints, experienced actors have always recognized the advantages of influencing policy outputs

1. "Institutional Change and the Quasi-Invisible Hand," *Journal of Law and Economics* 17 (Oct. 1974): 463.

2. Cited in Mark Blaug, *Economic Theory in Retrospect*, 3d ed. (Cambridge: Cambridge University Press, 1979), 526.

by such indirect methods. Instead of dispersing resources in trying to secure favorable results piecemeal—whether a tariff increase, a less stringent safety or environmental standard, or a more favorable tax treatment—it is often more efficient and politically wiser to use those resources to influence the institutional mechanisms that will produce future streams of valued outcomes.

This is particularly true in new areas of public policy such as pollution or health regulation, where administrative arrangements, jurisdictional responsibilities, enforcement procedures, and even property rights (for example, between polluters and pollutees) are still in flux and hence particularly open to institution-changing strategies. Also, the technical nature of these issues and the uncertainty surrounding the scientific basis of regulation promise large rewards to successful attempts to manipulate the flow of information or to change cognitive and cultural paradigms. Finally, rules that facilitate the formation of coalitions and the control of "free riders" assume great strategic importance where there are large numbers of potential actors with only limited stakes in the policy outcomes.

The situation of policy actors engaged in institutional change is not unlike that of participants in a new game when they discuss the rules under which the game should be played; or, to use another analogy, that of a group of individuals who meet to choose a constitution that specifies the powers of government and the basic rights of citizens. Although these analogies cannot be taken too literally—policy actors, unlike players or people engaged in constitutional choice under a Rawlsian "veil of ignorance," can usually anticipate which institutional arrangements will benefit them, at least on average—they serve to emphasize the qualitative difference between considerations relevant to institutional choice and those relevant to individual decisions within given institutional constraints. While the decision makers of the traditional model of rational choice attempt to maximize their goals within the rules set by the political and social environment, actual policy actors tend to view the rules of the game as possible targets of political action.

The main targets of institution-changing behavior are procedural rules for debating issues, setting agendas, reaching decisions, and implementing them, rather than substantive rules prohibiting or commanding particular actions—for instance, rules about how and by whom environmental standards should be set, rather than particular numerical values for those standards. Hence, the results of institutional change cannot be evaluated with reference to discrete, isolated decisions, but must be assessed in terms of sequences of interdependent decisions taken by a variety of actors over a period of time. This assumption of continuing relationships among policy actors introduces a temporal dimension that is absent in the one-time choice situations usually considered in policy analysis.

Procedural rules are especially important where enforcement must in the end rest on the consent of all the parties concerned, as in the international arena where there is no sovereign capable of enforcing compliance with substantive rules. Under such circumstances, who decides is often a more important question than what is decided, and indirect benefits, such as the recognition of one's role as a participant in the decision-making process, tend to loom larger than the immediate benefits that may result from individual decisions.[3]

The following example illustrates the importance of institutional choice in policy-making. After President Richard Nixon's unilateral decision to terminate the gold convertibility of the dollar in 1971, there was widespread feeling in Washington that the United States should launch a major initiative for reforming the international monetary system. The existing mechanisms for conducting negotiations did not seem adequate, however. Any major reform would most likely take the form of amendments to the charter of the International Monetary Fund (IMF). This suggested that the negotiations should be based within the framework provided by IMF. But locating the negotiation forum directly within IMF presented several problems. First, the board of governors, the IMF's policy-making body, was too unwieldy for conducting extensive negotiations and had no provision for

---

3. Kenneth W. Dam, *The Rules of the Game* (Chicago: University of Chicago Press, 1982), 4.

meetings at the level of deputies, that is, senior civil servants. Second, the executive directors were closely associated with the staff of the IMF; in fact, some of the directors felt themselves more officials of the fund than representatives of their own governments. If the executive board were the negotiation forum, then the fund staff would provide the secretariat function, and the preparatory work and background studies might be biased toward solutions that enhanced the role of the fund.

Another possible forum was the Group of Ten (G-10), the caucus of finance ministers of the ten major industrialized countries of the West: the United States, Canada, Japan, Great Britain, France, Germany, Italy, Belgium, Netherlands, and Sweden. The G-10 had already discussed several reform proposals and had in fact provided a principal forum for discussions leading to the Smithsonian agreement of December 1971, when an agreed realignment of exchange rates was achieved. However, from the American point of view there were two decisive objections to basing the reform negotiations in the G-10. First, the G-10 entirely excluded the less-developed countries, whose consent to a fundamental reform was indispensable, since any such reform would require amendment of the IMF charter and the less-developed countries collectively had enough votes to prevent ratification of any amendments that they did not endorse.

The second objection to using this group as the negotiation forum was the fear of U.S. negotiators of being outvoted by Europeans. Five of the ten countries were members of the European Economic Community and usually reached a common position before meetings. With the entry into the community of Great Britain, the Common Market countries would have a majority in the G-10.

The forum question was finally resolved by creating an ad hoc committee within the framework of the IMF. This new group became known as the Committee of Twenty (C-20) because of its membership of twenty countries or groups of countries. Each country or group of countries with an executive director in the IMF was entitled to membership in the C-20. Consequently, membership in the group was as broad as that of the fund and thus permitted participation by less-developed countries, as well as by those developed countries that were excluded from the G-10. The effect of the creation of C-20 was to move the negotiations out of the fund proper, thereby reducing the influence of the IMF staff and making it difficult for it to become an independent force in the negotiations. The negotiations would not be handled by the executive directors of the fund, but rather at the ministerial and senior subcabinet level among governments. A five-man bureau was to carry out the secretariat function in lieu of the fund staff. In this way, the U.S. government achieved what it wanted, namely, a forum in which its economic and financial power could not be offset by procedural means, and where the agenda and flow of information could not be manipulated by the IMF staff.[4]

ANALYZING INSTITUTIONAL CHANGE

Processes of institutional change are extremely complex. To avoid getting lost in details it is important to focus attention on a small set of key variables: (a) the group of actual and potential policy actors; (b) the resources available to them under different institutional arrangements, including (c) the amount and quality of information, skills, and expertise available to the various actors; and (d) environmental factors and constraints such as existing policies, societal values, ideologies, public opinion, and cognitive paradigms.[5]

In a simplified version of the model of institutional change, which still resembles the traditional model of rational choice, one would assume that policy actors act independently or in monolithic coalitions, like the unitary policymaker of decisionism or the consumers and the firms of neoclassical economic theory; that they have a single, homogeneous resource (money or po-

4. This account is based on the following sources: Dam, *The Rules of the Game*; George P. Shultz and Kenneth W. Dam, *Economic Policy Beyond the Headlines* (New York: W. W. Norton, 1977); and John Williamson, *The Failure of World Monetary Reform, 1971–1974* (New York: New York University Press, 1977).

5. The model of institutional change discussed here has been developed by Victor Goldberg in the article cited above, n. 1.

litical power); that information is imperfect and unequally distributed among the different actors but is not subject to manipulation; and that the political, social, and cultural environment is taken as given. Under these assumptions, marginal analysis leads to the conclusion that each actor should allocate his resources in such a way that the expected marginal return of the last unit of resource spent on influencing institutional arrangements in any particular policy area will be roughly equal to the benefit of the last unit of resource spent on any other type of influence or on the acquisition of some particular policy output.

As these assumptions are relaxed, more complex patterns of group behavior can be incorporated in the model. Consider first the assumption that organizations or interest groups act as a single individual in pursuit of their goals. In fact, collective action is seldom unitary and always confronts the "free rider" problem. For example, safer and healthier working conditions represent a public good that benefits all employees, regardless of union membership. Similarly, a better environment benefits everyone living in a given area independent of their direct contribution to environmentalist causes. In this way, actual or potential group members have incentives to be free riders. If the amount of resources available to a group depends significantly on its ability to induce or coerce its members to contribute to the common goal, the group leadership will try to obtain rules that facilitate joint action on certain issues. For example, unions may attempt to obtain legislation making safety and health issues mandatory subjects for collective bargaining. The possibility of class-action suits against polluters, or against employers in the case of occupational health, facilitates collective action by reducing the cost of using the courts to enforce claims. Important institutional changes, such as the environmental legislation of the 1970s, may even create opportunities around which new forms of collective action can be organized.

Moreover, any particular institutional arrangement affects the power and influence of various actors differently. Thus, placing the negotiations for international monetary reform within the Committee of 20, the institutional arrangement favored by the secretary of the treasury, also placed leadership of the U.S. negotiating team in the Treasury Department. The C-20 was a committee of the International Monetary Fund and the Treasury traditionally handled relations between the fund and the U.S. government. Had some other forum been chosen, it would have been conceivable for the State Department or even the Federal Reserve to lead the international monetary negotiations.

In turn, control of negotiations would have affected the outcomes because of the different policy perspectives of the various agencies of the American government. The Federal Reserve, being in constant contact with foreign central bankers, tended to share their views of the value of gold and fixed exchange rates. Similarly, the State Department was particularly sensitive to the diplomatic problems posed by any radical reform of the monetary system. The Treasury Department, on the other hand, was more concerned with the constraints that a return to fixed exchange rates and a U.S. commitment to gold convertibility might have on domestic economic policy. Hence, it tended to favor floating exchange rates—the regime eventually legitimated by the IMF at the Jamaica meeting in June 1974. Thus, institutional arrangements not only determine who decides, but also influence what is decided.

Consider now the nature of the resources available to the policy actors. In the policy arena many resources other than money (for example, votes, political influence, expertise, and information) are important; moreover, these resources are unequally distributed among the different actors. Less widely appreciated is the fact that the comparative advantage that various types of resources give to their owners depends on institutional factors. Any given institutional framework tends to favor some resources over others. For example, environmental and occupational health regulations affect the nature of property rights, reducing the power of private capital relative to political influence. Rule changes can create new resources, as well as affect the value of existing ones. Financial support for public participation in regulatory proceedings, or membership in advisory committees and administrative bodies, are examples. Policy actors accordingly will attempt to achieve institutional changes that either give them new resources or increase the value of those they already have. Also, the information available to the policy actors is unevenly distributed. As N. A. Ashford writes,

> Inequality of access—for example, between management and labor or between large firms and small ones—creates incentives for special interests to withhold or distort potentially damaging (or beneficial) information. Differential access converts information into a bargaining advantage for the more knowledgeable party, and compounds the difficulties of public and private decision-makers who must evaluate the merits of a bewildering variety of conflicting claims. Thus the phenomenon of differential access to information transforms the purely scientific and technical realm of information generation, dissemination and utilization, to the "political" arena.[6]

It follows that policy actors have incentives to invest resources in restructuring the channels through which information is collected, evaluated, and disseminated. For example, the ability to influence the institutional setting or the composition of research bodies and advisory boards may significantly affect the kind of data that are collected or the way in which they are evaluated. Even the scientific rules of evidence can become a subject of controversy in the policy arena, as shown by the debate concerning the regulation of the chemical pesticides Aldrin and Dieldrin discussed in chapter 2. The industry experts, it will be recalled, defined a carcinogen as a substance that increases the incidence of malignant tumors and required conclusive proof of the causal mechanism relating the tumors to the substance. On the other hand, according to the scientists who argued the case against A/D for EPA, even induction of benign tumors was sufficient to characterize a chemical as a carcinogen. Moreover, the EPA experts insisted that they were not required to produce evidence of causal mechanisms of carcinogenicity.

Strict criteria of scientific proof imply that fewer regulatory actions can be taken and facilitate legal challenges of regulatory decisions. For this reason, advocates and opponents of regulation tend to support different standards of proof.

6. *Crisis in the Workplace* (Cambridge: MIT Press, 1976), 16.

Similarly, those who argue that regulatory measures should be based on health criteria alone, regardless of cost, support the view that no safe levels of exposure to toxic and other dangerous substances exist. Those concerned with the cost of regulation, on the other hand, stress the adaptability and resilience of the human organism. These two views are based on different conceptions of a state of health: in one case it is assumed that no threat to health exists as long as the exposure does not induce a disturbance that overloads the normal protective mechanisms of the body; in the other, the assumption is that any concentration, however small, places an undesirable toxic or nuisance stress on the organism.

Neither position can be dismissed as being unreasonable or contrary to known biological laws; a state of health is a cultural rather than an empirical notion. The policy implications of adopting one or the other notion, however, are quite different. Hence, it is not surprising that policy actors devote resources to altering cultural norms and public attitudes toward health and the environment.

In sum, the cultural milieu is not viewed simply as a constraint but as a target for persuasion, propaganda, and political action. Interested parties struggle to impose their definition of the problem and of the instruments appropriate to its resolution. Changes from one set of conceptualizations or causal explanations to another carry important institutional implications as they determine which organizations are charged with obligations and opportunities for attacking the problem.[7]

INSTITUTIONAL CHANGE: A CASE STUDY

The passage of the U.S. Occupational Safety and Health Act (OSH Act) is a particularly clear illustration of the way in which actors attempt to influence policy outcomes by roundabout methods of institutional change.

7. Joseph R. Gusfield, *Drinking-Driving and the Symbolic Order* (Chicago: University of Chicago Press, 1981), 40–47.

The OSH Act, passed by Congress in 1970, is the first comprehensive attempt by the federal government to assure safe and healthful conditions for American workers. Prior to the passage of the act, the federal government's involvement in the regulation of occupational health and safety was limited to certain industries (such as mining, construction, and maritime) and certain businesses with federal contracts; the primary regulation of industry was at the state level. As in the case of much environmental regulation of the early 1970s, Congress reacted to widespread claims that state enforcement was ineffective and to the lack of uniform safety and health standards.

The agency responsible for administering the provisions of the act is the Occupational Safety and Health Administration (OSHA), located within the Department of Labor. OSHA is required to set occupational safety and health standards, and to conduct inspections at workplaces to ensure compliance with the standards and with the "general duty" obligation of employers in all cases not covered by specific standards.

Two more agencies have been established under the OSH Act: the Occupational Safety and Health Review Commission, a quasi-judicial review board that rules upon all challenged enforcement actions of OSHA; and the National Institute for Occupational Safety and Health (NIOSH), a research body located within the Department of Health, Education, and Welfare (now the Department of Health and Human Services). NIOSH is responsible for developing the scientific basis of occupational safety and health standards, and for making recommendations to OSHA.

The agency may promulgate a standard on its own initiative, in response to petitions of employees or employers, or in response to the recommendations of NIOSH. It is interesting to note that from about 1940 to the passage of the OSH Act, private organizations like the American Conference of Governmental Industrial Hygienists (ACGIH) played a major role in the development of occupational health standards. These were voluntary or "consensus standards," however.

Instead, under the new legislation, standards and other regulations requiring employers to eliminate specific conditions judged unsafe or unhealthy have the force of law. In fact, such is the importance of standards in the regulatory philosophy of the OSH Act that a former assistant secretary of labor for occupational safety and health has characterized it as "essentially a labor standards law. . . . Its heart is the development and enforcement of safety and health standards."[8] This explains the political importance of two questions which at first sight seem to have only technical or procedural significance: who should set and implement the standards, and how should the standards be set?

On the first issue there had been considerable debate in Congress prior to passage of the act. In House and Senate bills introduced in August 1969 and again in September 1970, the Republicans had proposed that authority for setting and enforcing standards be vested in a new National Occupational Safety and Health Board, whose members were to be appointed by the President. According to Democratic bills introduced in January 1969, and March 1970, the secretary of labor should set and enforce standards. In December 1970 a joint Senate and House conference committee worked out a final version of the conflicting bills. Since unions traditionally considered the Labor Department their natural ally in Washington, the jurisdictional issue was of the utmost importance to them. According to the Nader report on occupational health, "The pressure from the unions bore down on the issue of who should set the standards. In order to reach this goal, the unions were willing to make certain concessions."[9]

In the resulting compromise, the secretary of labor was given standard-setting and enforcement authority, while a quasi-judicial Occupational Safety and Health Review Commission received authority to exercise final administrative review of enforcement cases. According to section 12(a) and (b) of the act, the commission is composed of three members appointed by the President for terms of six years.

8. Quoted in Ashford, *Crisis in the Workplace*, 56.

9. Joseph Page and Mary-Win O'Brien, *Bitter Wages* (New York: Grossman, 1973), 178.

The second issue, concerning the criteria to be used in setting standards, received much less attention in the phase preceding passage of the act. Under section 6(b)(5), a standard for a toxic material must be set at the level.

> which most adequately assures, to the extent feasible, on the basis of the best available evidence, that no employee will suffer material impairment of health or functional capacity even if such an employee has regular exposure to the hazard dealt with by such a standard for the period of his working life.... In addition to the attainment of the highest degree of health and safety protection for the employee, other considerations shall be the latest available scientific data in the field, the feasibility of the standards, and experience gained under this and other health and safety laws.

This is the only place in the statute where the "feasibility" requirement appears. According to Doniger,[10] the requirement was added to section 6(b)(5) by the Senate committee on the suggestion of Senator Jacob Javits. In his individual views attached to the report, the senator explained: "As a result of this amendment, the Secretary, in setting standards, is expressly required to consider feasibility of proposed standards. This is an improvement over [the section without the amendment], which might be interpreted to require absolute health and safety in all cases, regardless of feasibility."[11]

The appropriateness of the term *feasibility* in this context is highly debatable, but the comments of Senator Javits make clear the real purpose of the clause—to induce OSHA to consider the costs of regulation in setting health standards.

The role of the states in regulating occupational health and safety was another important point of contention. National labor organizations were probably the most determined opponents of state regulation. The reasons of this opposition have been summarized by Ashford:

10. David D. Doniger, *The Law and Policy of Toxic Substances Control* (Baltimore: Johns Hopkins University Press, 1978), 39–40.

11. Quoted by Doniger, *Toxic Substances Control*, 40.

(1) The national unions will not be able to exercise sufficient influence at the state level, since (a) management organizations are relatively more powerful there, (b) local unions lack the expertise and manpower to be active, and (c) grassroots worker support for occupational health and safety issues is just beginning to be significant, but the effectiveness of local leadership does not yet compare to that of the more policy-oriented national union leadership. (2) The poor record of the states prior to the OSH Act gives support to the belief that the states will not do a good job. (3) Whatever the arguments are for state takeover with regard to safety, the states do not have the research capability necessary to tackle the more severe and prevalent occupational health problems.[12]

National union leaders are well aware of the difficulties of achieving safety and health benefits through collective bargaining. Issues concerning working conditions tend to have low priority in the bargaining agenda since financial gains are of more immediate interest to workers and their local representatives. Hence, federal legislation in this area strengthens the position of the union leadership with respect to the rank and file and to the unorganized members of the work force. The following statement made by one union leader in an interview with John Mendeloff is revealing: "The restraints on collective bargaining are very obvious; we don't have the power to get that stuff from management. Collective bargaining could be used more, but people tend to see themselves as impotent. OSHA helps to focus on the problem; how else could you get national attention to the problem of setting a level for some new material like vinyl chloride?"[13] This explains why by 1970 a bill on occupational safety and health had become one of the top legislative priorities of union leadership. Moreover, since regulation in this field was to be done mostly by means of standards, it was important that standard-setting authority be vested in a federal agency that labor viewed as "its" department, namely, the Department of Labor.

Activist groups such as Ralph Nader's Health Research Group

12. *Crisis in the Workplace*, 252.
13. John Mendeloff, *Regulating Safety* (Cambridge: MIT Press, 1979), 16.

and the Environmental Defense Fund fully shared labor's doubts about the willingness and capability of the states to provide adequate protection in the area of occupational health. The notion of giving priority to the quality of working conditions over the traditional wage goals of collective bargaining was also very much in line with the basic philosophy of the environmental movement. In addition, the shift of regulatory authority from the state to the federal level would produce significant economies of scale in the acquisition of influence by such means as lobbying and negotiations. Since some minimum threshold expenditures (for example, to hire a professional staff) must be made before effective action becomes possible, national public-interest groups have a clear interest in concentrating their efforts in Washington rather than diffusing them in fifty state capitols.

Finally, both labor and activist groups felt that the expertise available to industry in occupational health and safety could be matched only by a heavy presence of the federal government in this area. On a number of occasions, representatives of organized labor and activist groups have expressed the need to compensate the limited research capabilities of their organizations by relying more on federal research institutions. The OSH Act seemed to offer a number of interesting possibilities in this direction, through the creation of the National Institute for Occupational Safety and Health and of advisory bodies whose membership included representatives of labor and of the public.

Traditionally, business groups have vigorously opposed any direct federal role in matters of safety and health in the workplace, arguing that this is a state function. It has already been mentioned that prior to the passage of the OSH Act in 1970, occupational health standards were mostly developed by unofficial groups like the American Conference of Governmental Industrial Hygienists and the American National Standards Institute, and voluntarily adopted by industry as "consensus standards" or guidelines for good engineering practice.

The OSH Act has changed the concept of occupational health standards in three significant ways. First, the national standards are now legally enforceable. Second, standards promulgated by OSHA are no longer expressed only in terms of exposure limits but include medical examinations, labeling of hazardous containers and areas, work practices for hazard control (including the use of protective equipment and clothing), notification of employees of hazards to which they are exposed at the workplace, and monitoring and keeping records of environmental sampling. Finally, recommended standards must be based on publicly available information that may be evaluated by anyone, including union representatives and other interested parties.

Clearly, such changes imply heavier costs for industry; stricter regulations amount to a significant redefinition of property rights. Yet industry's interest in mounting a determined resistance to a federal takeover should not be exaggerated. For one thing, even the old decentralized system of regulation was becoming increasingly stringent. Pressures from ACGIH and other professional groups, and from the states, to reduce to a minimum worker exposure to carcinogens and other substances had been increasing since the early 1960s. Moreover, interstate variations in the stringency of regulation threatened to introduce unfair competitive advantages for companies located in certain states, while complicating the administrative problems of compliance for firms operating in several states.

Most important, industry must have realized, more clearly than other parties, the enormous difficulties of setting and implementing defensible occupational health standards. The basic difficulties are of two types. First, the lack of a firm scientific foundation on which such standards could be based. As already indicated in chapter 1, the major issues in setting health standards (for example, the choice of dose-response functions or extrapolations from animal experiments) are "trans-scientific" and thus allow considerable discretion in interpreting results.

The second difficulty concerns the very nature of standards as policy tools. Voluntary standards and guidelines, such as those issued by the ACGIH and NIOSH, can be determined on the basis of "health only" criteria, since they are not meant to be regulatory instruments but rather to supply scientific inputs to subsequent decisions. Mandatory standards, on the other hand, are policy tools and as such must include, more or less explicitly, considerations of costs and benefits. Typically, estimates of economic impacts will be at least as uncertain as estimates of safe dose levels and other biological parameters.

To take full advantage of the possibility for dilatory tactics inherent in the scientific and economic uncertainties, industry needed only a few and apparently minor changes in the language of the statute. One such change was the "feasibility" requirement added to section 6(b)(5) of the OSH Act by the Senate committee at the suggestion of Senator Javits. Other procedural requirements, like the publication in the *Federal Register* of proposed standards and the possibility of petition for judicial review, can also be effectively used to delay regulatory action. As a result, during its first nine years of existence OSHA promulgated only ten new standards: three between 1970 and 1974 (for asbestos, vinyl chloride, and a group of fourteen carcinogens), one in 1976 (for coke ovens), and six in 1976 (for lead, arsenic, DBCP, cotton dust, acrylonitrile, and benzene).

For example, in the case of the vinyl chloride (VC) standard set in 1974, industry opposed the proposed level of 1 part per million (ppm) on the grounds that OSHA lacked sufficient evidence on the harmfulness of VC at low doses; that it was technologically impossible for plants producing VC to meet the 1 ppm ceiling; and that the cost of approaching the ceiling would force the companies out of business. Subsequent experience was to show that meeting the 1 ppm standard was not as difficult or costly as industry had predicted. The convenient elasticity of the feasibility requirement has been aptly described by David Doniger in a detailed case study of the VC standard: "OSHA's statements and actions suggest that it was following an unarticulated principle that a standard is not feasible if it would cause more than slight changes in the number of firms in an industry, or in an industry's profit and growth rates, its output, and competitive position."[14]

A number of trade associations watch OSHA's activities closely: the American Industrial Health Council, an organization expressly created to oversee the process of OSHA rule making; the Society of Plastic Industries, which has been particularly active

14. *Toxic Substances Control*, 65.

in opposing the VC standard; and the American Petroleum Institute, the organization that defeated OSHA on the benzene standard. The standard was invalidated by the Court of Appeals for the Fifth Circuit on 5 October 1978, on the grounds that OSHA had failed to make quantitative estimates of the benefits of the standard and weigh them against the costs to see if the balance was "reasonable."

What about the position of the regulatory bureaucracy? An expanded federal role in the area of occupational safety and health means, of course, an increase in budget, employment levels, and political power for the federal bureaucracy. However, it was not difficult to guess that the financial and political costs of implementing occupational standards were likely to be high. There were precedents. In the case of air pollution control, for example, the Public Health Service had been unwilling, in the mid-1950s, to become involved in the problems of abatement and control. The health service apparently realized that serious efforts to determine dangerous levels of air pollution would lead to controversy, especially if it would have a role in recommending air quality or emission standards.[15]

The prospects for enforcing occupational health regulation must have been even more alarming. Consequently, the possibility given by the OSH Act to the states to develop and enforce their own standards, under OSHA's supervision, was compatible with the interests of the federal bureaucracy. According to Ashford, by early 1974 OSHA policy was to monitor state plans rather than continue federal enforcement activities when states with approved plans began to enforce standards.[16] It is easy to see that from OSHA's point of view this was an optimal strategy, since it minimized the agency's political costs, while giving it considerable control over the states.

According to section 18(c) of the act, acceptable state plans must meet a number of specifications whose purpose is to ensure that state standards and implementation procedures (including

15. Richard J. Tobin, *The Social Gamble* (Lexington, Mass.: Lexington Books, 1979), 34.

16. *Crisis in the Workplace*, 301.

right of entry and inspection without prior notice) be "at least as effective" as federal standards and procedures. Once a state plan has been approved, the secretary of labor is required to make a continuing evaluation of the state's performance and to withdraw approval for substantial failure to comply; OSHA provides 50 percent of the funds to run the state's program. In this way, all the political and half of the financial costs of implementation could be shifted to the states. At the same time, labor unions and public-interest groups were told that a state's standards and enforcement procedures would go just as far as federal efforts toward reducing accidents and deaths in the workplace.

The vagueness of the statutory language in connection with the approval of state plans increases OSHA's bargaining position with respect to state bureaucracies. Interpretation of the "at least as effective" requirement is necessarily subjective, even when applied to such specific items as exposure levels and number of inspectors. In the case of the "general duty" clause it becomes practically impossible to determine objectively whether state performance is at least as effective as federal performance. Consequently, the monitoring systems give a great deal of discretionary authority to OSHA, and in particular to the assistant regional directors for occupational safety and health.

Not all states, however, have been eager to grasp the possibility for independent regulation offered to them by the law; at the time of this writing, only twenty-five states operate under OSHA-approved plans. Apparently, the 50 percent funding provided by the OSH Act does not seem sufficient to compensate for the technical and political difficulties of implementing mandatory occupational health standards. Thus, OSHA has been forced by the logic of the situation to unwillingly exercise its power and to become the target of sharp criticism from management, labor, activist groups, the Office of Management and Budget, and the President himself.

The central thesis of this chapter is that policy actors not only pursue their goals within existing institutional, political, and cultural constraints, but also strive to change these constraints in their favor. While the traditional model of rational choice assumes that people attempt to optimize within given rules, I suggest that the policy process becomes much more understandable if one assumes that actors view the rules of the policy game as possible targets of political action. Examples of rule-changing behavior have been seen in such diverse areas as bureaucratic competition to control international monetary negotiations and the efforts of different economic and political interests to structure in their favor the process for setting health and safety standards.

Far from being exceptional occurrences, attempts to modify procedural rules and other institutional constraints are so pervasive that no descriptive or prescriptive policy analysis can be complete that does not explicitly take institution-changing behavior into consideration. Consider, as a further example, the question of the appropriate levels of government to which different functions should be entrusted. Economists writing about "optimal decentralization" and "optimal allocation of jurisdictional responsibility" have focused on the correct matching of functions and institutions, and on people's behavioral responses to different jurisdictional boundaries.[17]

Their analytic conclusions may prove irrelevant in the long run, however, since people will not only adapt their behavior to the existing jurisdictions, but will try to modify jurisdictional lines or to bring about allocations of jurisdictional responsibilities which, in their opinion, will best serve their interests. Gerrymandering of electoral districts is an obvious example, but analogous forms of jurisdiction-changing behavior can be observed in many other areas. In the field of pollution control, for example, it has been found that "there are even a number of instances on record when inventive owners of manufacturing establishments combined to incorporate industrial enclaves as cities or villages, as a defensive measurement against the imposition of pollution controls."[18]

17. See, for example, R. L. Bish, *The Public Economy of Metropolitan Areas* (Chicago: Rand-McNally, 1971).

18. F. P. Grad, "Intergovernmental Aspects of Environmental Controls," in

Finally, it should be pointed out that while models of the institution-changing behavior of self-interested actors are richer than the traditional rational-actor models of policy-making, they contain no implication that the interaction of self-interests will necessarily result in socially acceptable solutions.[19] On the contrary, the resulting policy outcomes may be unsatisfactory for most or all of the actors—as shown by the example of occupational safety and health regulation in the United States. What such models do imply is that normative recommendations should not be based on assumptions of ideal behavior of policy actors but should take institution-changing strategies into account. Although such strategies do not completely determine policy outcomes—if this were the case there would be no role for policy analysis or room for policy-making—they are of sufficient importance that ignoring them would produce misleading policy advice.

M. R. Laska and J. Gerba, eds., *Managing the Environment* (Washington, D.C.: U.S. Government Printing Office, 1973), 332.

19. Goldberg, "Institutional Change and the Quasi-Invisible Hand."

SIX

Choosing among Policy Instruments: The Case of Pollution Control

As was shown in the last chapter, different institutional arrangements affect differently the position and power of various policy actors by altering the relative importance of the resources they possess. Hence, actors have an incentive to use their influence and persuasive skills to change those arrangements and to manipulate the cultural milieu in which they operate.

In the present chapter I argue that the influence of the institutional and cultural environment extends also to the choice, mode of operation, and performance of policy instruments. Because the same policy target may be reached by different means, the question of the comparative advantage of various instruments looms large in the literature of economics and policy analysis. Many authors write as if it were possible to base the choice of policy instruments exclusively on their technical properties. Unfortunately, this cannot be done.

To begin with, policy instruments are seldom ideologically neutral. For example, it is often difficult to distinguish between a preference for monetary instruments per se and a preference for the policy outlook of the monetary authorities. Similarly, many people view the choice between changing government spending and changing taxes as a means of regulating the economy in terms of their views about the proper size of government. Again, whether one prefers administrative measures or economic incentives to control pollution seems to depend at least as much on philosophy and ideology as on the technical properties of the two approaches. Those who favor the extension of market principles to previously nonpriced resources like air and water in the name of efficiency naturally prefer market-oriented regulatory instruments, while those who oppose the encroachment of utilitarian principles in social life tend to oppose them.

Nor are policy instruments distributionally neutral. The means governments use to fight inflation, unemployment, or pollution affect different social groups differently, and these distributional impacts may be regarded by both winners and losers as the main reason for supporting or opposing a particular instrument. Even technological alternatives, such as different methods of energy production, have important distributional implications. Operators and beneficiaries of a particular development will not only support it, but also attempt to gain a less constrained use of it through political persuasion and by manipulating the regulatory framework.

Third, instruments cannot be neatly separated from goals. As was noted in chapter 2, the choice of means helps to alter the criteria by which the correctness of the means must be judged. Also, policy goals are often defined in terms of the available means. Demonstrating that there is a problem which can be attacked by one's favorite instrument is a very real preoccupation of participants in the policy process. For example, according to Martha Derthick, the prevailing technique of policy analysis in the Social Security Administration in the 1950s and 1960s was to identify a social problem, such as lack of health care, and to develop arguments and methods for dealing with it through social insurance.[1] Moreover, as I mentioned in chapter 1, when goals are vague or ambiguous and outcomes difficult to measure, the instruments used acquire a significance that goes well beyond their purely instrumental value.

1. *Policymaking for Social Security* (Washington, D.C.: Brookings Institution, 1979), 159–63.

These objections to the notion that policy instruments are chosen exclusively or even primarily on the basis of their technical properties have been voiced frequently. In this chapter I focus on a different and more fundamental objection: the performance of instruments depends less on their formal properties than on the political and administrative context in which they operate. Institutional structures, rather than abstract theory, shape policy results.

THE IMPORTANCE OF CONTEXT

In constructing a theory it may be proper to disregard the institutional context in order to facilitate understanding of how an instrument would perform in an idealized situation. Formal theories of economic or environmental policy usually proceed in this fashion. But practical problems are always related to particular contexts and must be met by actions taken in certain specified situations. Unlike theorists, analysts are not free to make simplifying assumptions but must consider how policy instruments are effectively constrained by political, administrative, and other institutional factors—and by people's attempts to manipulate these factors in their favor.

A practical problem is not solved by offering a theoretical solution that does not take into consideration the limitations which the context imposes. Thus, it is quite misleading to employ ideal standards in evaluating or comparing alternative policy instruments; the standards must relate to the particular context in which the instruments are used. And because the context in which public policy is made includes values, norms, perceptions, and ideologies, technical considerations are insufficient as criteria of choice.

Since I will discuss and illustrate these propositions with reference to environmental policy-making, it is important to start by underlining their general significance. The school of economics known as "rational expectations," for instance, emphasizes the role of the institutional context in economic policy-making. These economists recognize that the economy cannot be treated like a piece of putty that can be molded and shaped by the model builders or policymakers to fulfill their vision of the public interest. Economic policy, they argue, is more than a straightforward application of economic theory; theory, policy, and institutional analysis are closely interrelated.[2]

Even before this belated appreciation of the political and institutional dimensions of economic policy, Milton Friedman had pointed out that it is impossible to choose among alternative methods of solving the economic problem solely in terms of the formal conditions for an optimal allocation of society's resources. This is because the formal conditions may be attained by different institutional arrangements that have important noneconomic consequences. As Pareto showed long ago, the equilibrium allocation of resources in a freely competitive society based on private property is identical with the allocation that a socialist state would attempt to achieve if it wished to maximize social welfare.

On a purely formal level, central planning could bring about the same allocation of resources as a market economy by solving the same system of simultaneous equations. In theory, this result could also be accomplished by other methods—for example, by a system of taxes and incentives so designed as to induce monopolists to set prices at the levels that would prevail under competitive conditions. These various approaches are abstractly equivalent in the sense that, given sufficient information and total institutional flexibility, they can be shown to produce an efficient allocation of the available resources.

This can only mean that economic efficiency is not sufficiently discriminating as a criterion of choice. In order to choose among different approaches, it is necessary to examine the particular institutional arrangements used to implement the abstract solutions, and hence to introduce additional noneconomic criteria like administrative and political feasibility.[3] Moreover, since none

2. Karl Brunner and Allan H. Meltzer, "Theory, Policy, Institutions: Papers from the Carnegie-Rochester Conference on Public Policy," in Brunner and Meltzer, eds., *Theory, Policy, Institutions* (Amsterdam: North-Holland, 1983).

3. Milton Friedman, *Essays in Positive Economics* (Chicago: University of Chicago Press, 1953), 301–19.

of the arrangements will be clearly superior, taking all the relevant criteria into consideration, persuasive arguments about the appropriate ranking of values—about the relative importance of freedom, wealth, efficiency, and equity—are certain to be at least as important as technical analyses in determining one's preferences.

As I show in the following pages, recent debates about alternative approaches to pollution control raise analogous, if less momentous, issues. In fact, in any area of public policy the choice of instruments, far from being a technical exercise that can be safely delegated to the experts, reflects as in a microcosm all the political, moral, and cultural dimensions of policy-making.

THE INSTRUMENTS OF ENVIRONMENTAL POLICY

The variety of tools available to environmental policymakers has been significantly enriched in recent years by a number of clever techniques, ranging from effluent charges to marketable emission permits. Yet legislators, bureaucrats, industrialists, and even environmentalists have shown little interest in the new instruments and continue to favor administrative methods (such as standards, prohibitions, and licenses) whose shortcomings have repeatedly been demonstrated.

In the few instances where more sophisticated tools have been used (for example, in France, the Netherlands, and Germany), they have supplemented, not replaced, the traditional approaches. Moreover, the new instruments have so far not produced the results predicted by theory, nor have they brought about the profound administrative changes anticipated by their advocates. The injection of new wine into old institutional bottles has not simplified but possibly complicated—and at any rate further expanded—an already complex regulatory framework.

The disappointment of the tool designers is understandable. Less justifiable is their failure to recognize the inadequacy of the model of policy-making implicit in their proposals. Thus, many analysts have lambasted the traditional administrative approach to pollution control for its inefficiency and its tendency to become

"a political process entailing bargaining between parties of un-
equal power."[4] They have repeatedly argued that effluent
charges would achieve environmental goals at the least social
cost, provide incentives to technical innovation, and, by their
automatism, reduce the scope for administrative discretion and
bargaining.[5]

These analysts have overlooked two important points. First,
as already noted, theoretically derived solutions are often compatible with quite different institutional arrangements. It makes
little sense to discuss the choice of policy instruments in an institutional vacuum, since their effectiveness cannot be estimated
without detailed knowledge of the institutional context in which
they will operate. Second, the same forces that influence and
"distort" the instruments of administrative regulation will also
attempt to bend other policy instruments; the model of institutional choice developed in chapter 5 applies also to this case.

Before arguing these points in detail it may be useful to review
the main instruments of pollution control. We start with emission
(or effluent) charges, which are fees, collected by the government, levied on each unit of pollutant emitted into the air or
water. Consider the familiar example of a chemical factory producing a product P and discharging its wastes into a nearby river
or polluting the air with its fumes. These discharges reduce the
quality of the environment and its suitability for a number of
alternative uses. Since water and air are common property, their
services (in this case the service of carrying off wastes) are not
sold. The cost in terms of reducing environmental quality is thus
overlooked by the price system; the failure to account for such
costs leads to an oversupply of P and an undersupply of the
benefits reduced by pollution. This is the efficiency problem. If
the damages caused by pollution were "internalized"—if polluters were charged the full costs of pollution—resource use would

    4. A. Myrick Freeman III, Robert H. Haveman, and Allen V. Kneese, *The
Economics of Environmental Policy* (New York: Wiley, 1974), 105.
    5. Ibid., 170. See also Robert and Nancy S. Dorfman, eds., *Economics of the
Environment: Selected Readings* (New York: W. W. Norton, 1972) and Allen V.
Kneese and Charles L. Schultze, *Pollution, Prices, and Public Policy* (Washington,
D.C.: Brookings Institution, 1977), 136.

become more efficient: the price of P would be higher, less P would be produced, and pollution would be abated. In theory, at least, efficiency can be restored by charging the chemical factory an emission or effluent fee on its discharges of pollutants.

As long as marginal damage costs are known, public authorities simply set the fee at a level equal to the marginal damage caused by each unit of waste. A cost-minimizing firm would then decrease its waste flows as long as the marginal cost of abatement was less than the fee for discharging, settling at the optimum where marginal treatment costs equal the fee.

If the determination of a socially optimal pollution charge presents few conceptual difficulties, the practical problems are staggering. Abatement costs vary greatly among firms, municipalities, and households, and the sheer number of polluters makes reliable estimates all but impossible to obtain. The situation is, if anything, even more difficult in the case of damage functions, where we must reckon with the practical impossibility of quantifying some of the basic values affected by pollution. Moreover, ecological damage varies not only with the type and level of activity, but also with the location of the polluting unit, time of discharge, changing meteorological conditions, and so on.

It is not surprising, therefore, that first-best but practically infeasible solutions have been generally abandoned in favor of second-best or satisfying solutions combining elements of the regulatory and the market approach. One such solution, known as the charges-and-standards approach, has been proposed by Baumol and Oates. It consists of assuming a given set of ambient standards (that is, the standards are taken to be determined exogenously through the political process), while the price system is put to use in the realization of the environmental constraints that society imposes on its activity. Specifically, the charges are to be selected so as to achieve given quality standards rather than attempting to base them on the unknown value of marginal net damages.[6]

6. William J. Baumol and Wallace E. Oates, *The Theory of Environmental Policy* (Englewood Cliffs, N.J.: Prentice-Hall, 1975).

Let us consider now another market approach to pollution control. The major difficulty in internalizing the costs of environmental pollution is the ambiguous specification of exchangeable property rights to media like air and water. J. H. Dales's proposal to establish a market in "pollution rights" is an interesting attempt to remove some of the ambiguity.[7] According to this proposal, the public authority does not attempt to tax polluters at a predetermined rate. Instead, it sets an upper limit L (in equivalent tons) to the amounts of discharge allowed into the environment of a region for a given period of time. (In Dales's proposal, water is the environmental medium.) It then issues L licenses ("pollution rights") and puts them up for sale, requiring everyone who discharges one equivalent ton of waste during, say, a year to hold one pollution right for the entire year. If L is less than the number of equivalent tons of waste currently being discharged, the rights will command a positive price, and a market will develop in response to the competition among buyers and sellers of pollution rights.

At least under static conditions, the outcome that theoretically prevails under a system of pollution rights can be made identical to the one that theoretically prevails under the charges-and-standards system. In fact, the market for pollution rights will generate an equilibrium price at the point where the capitalized value of the marginal cost of treating an extra pound of waste will be the same for all discharges in the same region, thus assuring that the environmental quality objective will be satisfied at a minimum total cost.

Implicit in what has been said so far is the assumption that the cost of reducing the damage inflicted by a polluting activity is less than the benefits created by the abatement—up to the equilibrium point at which the two exactly balance. Whenever this is the case, the possibility arises of a contractual solution to the pollution problem. That is, the pollutees can afford to pay the polluter enough to cover the abatement costs, and in such a way that the transaction is advantageous for all parties concerned.

7. *Pollution, Property, and Prices* (Toronto: University of Toronto Press, 1968).

As Ronald Coase has shown,[8] such a system of contractual payments (or "bribes," as they are often called) could in principle achieve the same result as a scheme of pollution charges. To see why this is so, consider a situation in which the pollution damage suffered by the inhabitants of the residential areas surrounding the factory increases monotonically with the level of output P. Suppose that a charge of ten dollars per unit of output would be required to cover the cost of the damage, and that raising the price of P by this amount reduces demand by, let us say, 20 percent. This reduced amount, at which social marginal cost is equal to price, becomes the most profitable output for the factory owner.

On the other hand, if there is no charge—if the manufacturer is not required by law to pay damages—the inhabitants might come together and agree to "bribe" him to reduce his output. Under our assumptions, the maximum they would be willing to pay is of course ten dollars per unit of (foregone) output—the amount of damage they would otherwise have to bear. By offering the manufacturer this much in compensation for each unit less of P he produces, they induce him to reduce output by exactly 20 percent. Beyond the 20 percent reduction of output, the gross profit per unit of P becomes greater than the payment of ten dollars, the maximum compensation the inhabitants can offer.

Of course, we may not approve of the redistribution of wealth arising from a voluntary contractual solution of the pollution problem. Leaving redistributive issues aside for the moment, note that the contractual solution will be practically feasible only if the number of parties involved is quite small. With many parties, the transaction costs of arranging and operating such a compensation system—the cost of getting together the people affected by the pollution, of assessing damage, and so on—may be prohibitive.

The familiar "free rider" problem must also be noted here.

8. "The Problem of Social Cost," *Journal of Law and Economics* 3 (Oct. 1960): 1–44.

Since it is technically difficult to exclude anyone from the benefits of reduced pollution, the incentive to contribute to the necessary payments is correspondingly reduced. Some assistance from the state to overcome the free rider problem seems necessary to make the contractual solution viable.

The instruments of pollution control discussed so far are market-oriented in the sense that they rely on economic incentives to produce the desired outcome. They are also new and largely untried.

Next we consider the traditional administrative approach. This relies on a wide variety of tools: standards, permits, licenses, prohibitions, and subsidies, to mention only a few. In addition, the government provides directly important environmental services like research, education, and the construction and operation of waste treatment plants or of reservoirs to augment water flows during low-flow periods. All these instruments have a role to play in a comprehensive environmental policy, but standards are probably the best-known tools and the ones most frequently used. They are also the main target of the criticism of the advocates of a market approach to regulation. For these reasons, the following discussion is focused on them.

In pollution control at least three different types of standards must be distinguished: specification (or technical) standards, ambient standards, and emission (or effluent) standards on particular sources of pollution.

When specification standards are used, polluters are told what kind of equipment or abatement strategies to adopt, such as requiring a utility to install stack gas scrubbers and/or burn low-sulfur fuel at a generating facility. Ambient standards express in quantitative form the qualitative goals of an environmental program. For instance, if the goal of the program is to achieve water suitable for recreational purposes, the ambient standard may prescribe that the dissolved oxygen (DO) content of the stream be above x percent at least y percent of the time. Effluent standards, on the other hand, state how much of certain types of pollutants are allowed from any given source (for instance, the amount of biochemical oxygen demand in pounds per day from a factory), where the exact amounts may be determined in a way to achieve the pollution abatement goal set by an ambient standard.

In comparing standards with effluent charges it is important to keep in mind that a system of standards includes not only constraints on certain kinds of undesirable behavior, but also penalties for failure to comply. The response of economic agents to a standard depends, at least in part, on the relationship between the costs of complying with the standard and the expected costs of violating it. Once this fact is recognized, the theoretical distinction between standards and charges becomes blurred. In fact, it has been shown that under certain assumptions charges can be translated into standards and standards into charges.[9]

CHARGES VERSUS STANDARDS

The statement that charges and standards are theoretically equivalent may sound paradoxical. If they are fungible policy instruments, why so much controversy over their respective merits? Have advocates and critics been arguing about words? Or perhaps theoretical arguments overlook some genuine but hard-to-formalize differences?

In attempting to answer these questions we shall proceed through several steps. First I will show that in an idealized world of perfect information, charges and standards are indeed equivalent, but only with respect to the single criterion of economic efficiency. Moving next to a more realistic situation where information is both costly and imperfect and administration costs cannot be neglected, we find that the best choice of instrument remains difficult to judge a priori. In the next section we review the experience of some European countries where pollution charges have been used for a number of years. We find that

9. Russell F. Settle and Burton A. Weisbrod, "Governmentally Imposed Standards: Some Normative Aspects," in Ronald G. Ehrenberg, ed., *Research in Labor Economics* (Greenwich, Conn.: JAI, 1978), 166–70. See also Allen V. Kneese and Blair T. Bower, *Managing Water Quality: Economics, Technology, Institutions* (Baltimore: Johns Hopkins University Press, 1968), 136.

actual systems differ so much from the conceptually pure case discussed in the textbooks that direct comparisons are practically impossible. Also, there is no evidence that the use of charges would reduce the role of administrative discretion and political bargaining. Finally, in the concluding section I argue that differences of opinion over policy instruments may be due less to factual disagreements over their theoretical properties than to ideological preferences and conflicts of interests. Readers who are not interested in a detailed comparison of charges and standards may proceed to the next section without loss of continuity.

In an ideal world, the policymaker has full information about the cost and damage functions of each economic unit. Armed with this knowledge, he can achieve a socially optimal level of pollution by setting the charge at the level where marginal abatement costs equal marginal damages. Note that since environmental damages depend on the assimilative capacity of the environment, which varies with type of effluent, location, time, and other factors, an efficient (least-cost) policy requires a system of nonuniform charges, rather than a single uniform charge for all polluters in a given area. If the policymaker knows the optimal level of pollution for each firm, he can also design a system of (nonuniform) effluent standards so as to equate the firms' marginal abatement costs. Thus, the optimal level of pollution can be achieved at least cost with a system of standards just as well as with a system of charges.

In the preceding discussion on alternative market approaches we have seen that in an ideal world of perfect information and zero transaction costs, a socially optimal solution can also be achieved by the method of saleable pollution rights, or by contractual payments. This shows that the complexity of the choice of instrument is lost when the only criterion is economic efficiency. Theoretically equivalent solutions can have quite different institutional and social implications. For example, the contractual solution assumes that environmental property rights are vested in the polluters, while the imposition of effluent charges implies that those rights are vested in the community. The contractual solution causes a redistribution of wealth from pollutees to polluters; charges force polluters to pay the community for permission to pollute. Both solutions are efficient but the distributional consequences are different.

Consider now the equivalence of charges and standards. Firms will tend to produce a higher level of output and offer greater employment when they are faced with a standard than when faced with an effluent charge. This is because a standard allows pollution up to a fixed limit free of charge, while charges impose a cost at all levels of pollution. Hence, the lower marginal cost of production under a system of standards will lead, everything else being equal, to higher levels of output and employment.[10] Because the social consequences of the two methods are different, one would have to weigh the greater uncompensated loss of environmental quality against the greater output and employment made possible by the standards approach. The efficiency criterion is not a sufficient criterion of choice in this case either.

Under more realistic conditions of limited information and positive transaction costs, a socially optimal level of pollution is not a feasible policy goal. One possible second-best policy is the already mentioned charges-and-standards approach, where charges are used to achieve an exogenously given ambient standard. It can be shown that a system of charges can reach the target at least cost, but the proof assumes that the charges are based not simply on the amount of pollution generated, but on the environmental damage caused by the pollution. If the damage depends on location and other factors, an efficient solution will require a system of individualized charges for each different source of pollution. In fact, in some situations a uniform charge could lead to a more costly solution than an effluent standard prescribing an equal percentage reduction of emissions by all polluters.[11] With more than sixty thousand industrial sources of water pollution in a country like the United States, a tailor-made

10. Paul Burrows, "Pricing Versus Regulation for Environmental Protection," in J. J. Culyer, ed., *Economic Policies and Social Goals* (New York: St. Martin's, 1974), 273–83.

11. Susan Rose Ackerman, "Effluent Charges: A Critique," *Canadian Journal of Economics* 6 (Nov. 1973): 512–28. See also Baumol and Oates, *The Theory of Environmental Policy*, 146.

system of charges would involve a prodigious amount of calculation and enormous administration costs.

In sum, as long as environmental quality depends on location and other factors that differ among polluters, only a system of individualized and correctly calculated charges has superior efficiency properties, and then only with respect to a uniform effluent standard. In principle, a tailor-made system of effluent standards would also allow diversity of treatment among different polluters, thus achieving the desired level of environmental quality at least cost. We may conclude with Clifford Russell that "there is very little choice between charge schemes and regulatory schemes, in principle, when the sole criterion is static efficiency."[12]

What about other criteria like effectiveness, administration costs, flexibility, and dynamic efficiency? Opinions among experts differ, partly because of a lack of data, partly because some necessary distinctions (for example, between different types of standards or of policy targets) are sometimes overlooked. It is true that, given any charge, profit-maximizing or cost-minimizing polluters will equate their marginal costs to the charge, so that the resulting reduction in pollution is achieved at least cost; but there is no guarantee that the charge will be sufficient to achieve the desired level of environmental quality. If the reduction actually obtained was not chosen in advance as the policy target, it is disingenuous to claim, after the fact, that it has been achieved efficiently. On the other hand, given an environmental objective and appropriate enforcement procedures, effluent standards can always be calculated so as to reach the target; but there is in general no way of knowing whether the objective will be achieved efficiently.

Predictability and speed of impacts are particularly important in some instances of rapidly changing environmental conditions that may pose a serious threat to public health (such as an atmospheric inversion which prevents the escape of pollutants) and

12. "What Can We Get from Effluent Charges?", in Robert H. Haveman and B. Bruce Zellner, eds., *Policy Studies Review Annual*, vol. 3 (Beverly Hills, Calif.: Sage, 1979), 264.

in the case of extremely hazardous pollutants. Even supporters of the charges approach agree that in such situations one cannot rely on pricing incentives to curtail emissions quickly and reliably; direct controls (prohibitions or standards) are much more dependable.

Concerning administration costs, it is obvious that waste discharges must be monitored under either system. However, the metering problem is especially serious for the charges approach, since an accurate estimate of average emission flows is necessary in order to calculate the total tax bill. The greater the variation in waste flows, the higher the costs of monitoring, since frequent samples will have to be taken at each source. Under a system of standards, the purpose of monitoring is simply to determine whether a threshold value has been exceeded. This simplifies measurement problems and sampling procedures, which only need to be sufficient to uncover a high percentage of violations. Thus, the differential in administration costs tends to favor the use of effluent standards rather than charges.

Finally, let us consider the claim that charges are superior to standards with respect to flexibility and because they provide an incentive to discover new, more efficient technologies for reducing pollution. One often hears that charges, in contrast to standards, leave firms free to choose their own best strategy to reduce pollution. But under a system of effluent (or performance) standards, firms are just as free to choose their best means of attaining the required amount of pollution abatement as they are under a charges system. The mistake is to confuse performance standards with specification standards that tell polluters what kind of equipment or abatement strategies to adopt. Here we are comparing effluent charges with effluent standards, not with standards in general.

The argument that charges provide a continuing incentive to search for better and cheaper ways of preventing pollution is more persuasive. Even analysts who are not convinced that charges are generally superior consider this incentive effect as probably the strongest argument in their favor.[13] By lifting the

13. See, for example, ibid., 253.

environment out of the category of free goods, charges encourage economy in the use of environmental inputs, even below the target level of pollution abatement. Effluent standards do not provide this incentive, since they allow pollution up to the prescribed level free of charge. However, this conclusion must be qualified in two ways. First, very strict standards, and prohibitions as a limiting case, can also be effective in channeling growth away from socially undesirable technologies and materials toward more acceptable forms of production. The ban of DDT and some toxicological standards, like those for vinyl chloride or asbestos, are examples. A second, and sometimes more important, qualification is that the incentive effect of charges can be seriously eroded by inflation. This is precisely what has happened in France, as will be seen in the next section. In an inflationary economy charges would have to be continually adjusted to maintain the desired relative prices of environmental inputs. Standards, on the other hand, represent a physical constraint on polluting activities and thus are not eroded by inflation (except for the financial penalties). Incidentally, saleable pollution rights also enjoy this advantage over charges since they are also fixed in physical terms.

The one clear conclusion that emerges from this survey is that the case for the superiority of pricing over administrative regulation for pollution control is far from conclusive. One possible exception to the verdict "not proven" is the incentive argument, but even here important qualifications must be added. The best choice of instrument remains difficult to judge on the basis of a priori reasoning. Does the empirical evidence suggest more definite conclusions?

EFFLUENT CHARGES IN PRACTICE

The experience of countries like France, the Netherlands, and Germany, where charges have been used for a number of years, has been often cited by American analysts as proof of the feasibility and distinctive superiority of the method. In order to assess these claims it is necessary to consider those national experiences both in their own terms and with reference to the theoretical model. Fortunately, a fairly extensive literature on pollution control in Europe is now available,[14] so that we only need to review those aspects that are directly related to the use of charges.

Effluent charges have been introduced in France by the 1964 Law on Water Management and Pollution Control (Loi relative au régime et à la repartition des eaux et à la lutte contre leur pollution). "Revolutionary" as this law appeared to distant American observers,[15] it did not in fact replace previous legislation. Rather, it created a new system on top of the old one based on permits issued by the prefect of the province (département) in which pollution would occur. The prefects have not only retained full control of the permit system, enforcement of the new law is largely in their hands.

Responsibility for the management of water quality is now divided between the traditional bureaucracy (prefects and the inspectorates of classified establishments) and the new structures created by the 1964 law: the National Water Committee (Comité National de l'Eau) at the national level and, at the basin level, the basin committees (comités de bassin) and the basin agencies (agences financières de bassin).

The National Water Committee has advisory functions. Its sixty members, each of whom is appointed by the prime minister for a term of six years, represent the users, the state, and elected local officials on an equal basis. Economic interests are strongly represented in the first group; polluters—firms, households, and municipalities—have a two-thirds majority.

---

14. Kneese and Bower, *Managing Water Quality*; Ralph W. Johnson and Garner M. Brown, Jr., *Cleaning up Europe's Waters* (New York: Praeger, 1976); Organization for Economic Co-operation and Development, *Pollution Charges in Practice* (Paris: OECD, 1980); Blair T. Bower, Remi Barre, Jochen Juhner, and Clifford S. Russell, *Incentives in Water Quality Management: France and the Ruhr Area* (Washington, D.C.: Resources for the Future, 1981); Paul B. Downing and Kenneth Hanf, eds., *International Comparisons in Implementing Pollution Laws* (The Hague: Kluwer-Nijhoff, 1983).

15. Kneese and Bower, *Managing Water Quality*, 270.

Industrial interests are favored even more in the basin committees, which are primarily advisory bodies but whose approval is required to determine the basis of calculation and the level of the charges proposed by the basin agencies. The categories of users represented in the committees, and the number of seats attributed to each category, vary somewhat from basin to basin, but "the interests connected with industry, broadly interpreted, carry considerable weight in all the committees, approaching or exceeding half the users' representation. This is in perfect agreement with the logic of the 1964 law, since industrialists have the primary responsibility for pollution and are the ones most affected by the charges."[16]

Pollution charges are set (or, rather, proposed) by the basin agencies. Of the sixteen members of the executive board of each agency, eight are from the national administration, while the remaining seats are divided between local administrators and different groups of users.[17] Because charges cannot be set without the approval of the basin committees, this smaller representation of industrial interests does not change the general impression of the law's favorable treatment of industrial polluters. One of the criticisms of the agencies has been that they are under the policy control of basin committees dominated by representatives of various polluter groups, who are understandably reluctant to raise the charges to "incentive level" rates.[18]

In spite of this dependence, the basin agencies must be considered the keystone of the new system. They elaborate multiannual programs of pollution control, set charges on the basis of the costs of those programs, and grant subsidies and loans to firms for investment in pollution abatement equipment. They are not responsible for monitoring and enforcement, however. Basin agency officials feel that enforcement is generally ineffec-

16. Alain Fenet, "L'Administration de l'eau en France", *Revue administrative* 26 (July-Aug. 1973): 390.
17. There are now six basin agencies in France: Artoy-Picardie, Seine-Normandie, Loire-Bretagne, Ardour-Garonne, Rhône-Méditerranée-Corse, and Rhin-Meuse.
18. Johnson and Brown, *Cleaning up Europe's Waters*, 65.

tive, in part because the prefects, who control most of the sanctions, are concerned more with political support than with pollution control.

The existing institutional framework and the political power of the prefects have left very little space for the creation of adequate mechanisms for coordinating the permit and the charge systems.[19] Even in the land of Cartesian clarity the policymaker is not free to write on a clean slate. The mixture of old and new has resulted in a motley array of arrangements for issuing licenses and of technical and economic controls, including some brave attempts to use sophisticated economic tools like shadow programming on the lines of the French economic plan.[20]

Such attempts have created the impression in some outside observers that the basin agencies have "an absolutely clear objective—economic efficiency in the full sense of the term. The aim is to establish a system in which the incremental costs of further improvement of water quality balance the incremental benefits, and in which the full range of alternative ways of improving water quality can be assessed and all measures brought into optimal balance."[21] In reality, the French system bears little resemblance to the textbook model and can hardly claim to be economically efficient. Charges are based on flows discharged rather than on biological and environmental damages, as required by theory. Moreover, the amount of pollution produced by a firm is estimated on the basis of pollution coefficients ascribed to the entire industry to which the firm belongs. This uniformity of treatment, combined with a very low level of charges, does not provide incentives to technical innovation in pollution abatement, or even to adopting already available technologies for preventing pollution.

19. Heinz Schleicher, "Building Coordination Structures," in Franz-Xavier Kaufmann, Giandomenico Majone, and Vincent Ostrom, eds., *Guidance, Control, and Evaluation in the Public Sector* (Berlin: Walter DeGruyter, 1986), 511–30.

20. Jean-Phillipe Barde, "An Examination of the Polluter-Pays Principle Based on Case Studies," in Organization for Economic Co-operation and Development, *The Polluter-Pays Principle* (Paris: OECD, 1975), 100.

21. Kneese and Bower, *Managing Water Quality*, 283.

In 1979 French charges were lower than Dutch charges by a factor of 6 to 15, and because they are not indexed, attempts to raise them have been nullified by inflation. For example, in the Seine-Normandie basin (the most populated, urbanized, and industrialized of the six water basins), the charge per population equivalent, when expressed in current francs, was 3.75 in 1972 and 4.41 in 1975. In constant francs, however, the charge was 2.81 in 1972 and only 2.04 in 1975.[22]

The main purpose of charges is to raise funds to finance the pollution control programs elaborated by the agencies. However, these revenues cover only a fraction of the total costs, so that the officially accepted principle that polluters should pay for the cost of removing the damage they cause is systematically violated. The well-founded expectation that charges would be kept low and that generous subsidies and aids would be forthcoming probably explains the lack of serious opposition of French industry to the new system. This has increased the system's political acceptability, but at the cost of a serious loss in static and dynamic efficiency.

The general approach of the basin agencies seems to be inspired more by their intuition of what is politically feasible than by technical analyses and economic calculations. Contrary to the expectation of some American economists that a system of charges "would reduce the scope for administrative discretion and bargaining,"[23] bargaining and negotiations play a major role in the French system. The basic formula used for the determination of the charges, for example, has been adopted only after extensive consultation with various interest groups and is more meaningful in political than in economic or scientific terms.[24]

It has also been claimed that the charges approach "would resolve most of the political conflict over the environment in a highly visible way where those who would be hurt by such policy

22. OECD, *Pollution Charges in Practice*, 37.
23. Freeman, Haveman, and Kneese, *The Economics of Environmental Pollution*, 105.
24. Johnson and Brown, *Cleaning up Europe's Waters*, 47–48.

could see what was happening."[25] However, a French observer has characterized the approach of the basin agencies as "common sense, somewhat akin to that of a friendly society where the users contribute to the cost of the development which they have decided to carry out together."[26] In a friendly society the tendency to limit the size of the dues to be paid is strong. Hence, it is not surprising that, on average, the rates of charges per population equivalent account for only one-third of the unit cost for treatment plants.

Before going on to consider briefly the Dutch and German systems, we may sum up the French case by quoting the conclusions of a detailed study of the institutional aspects of water management in France:

> Being inspired by an economic rationality accepted by all the interested parties, the...programs of the agencies have often been considered capable of starting a chain of solutions acceptable to everybody.... Administrative responsibilities had only to align themselves to the solutions worked out by the economists. This hope, widely shared at the time of the creation of the basin structures, has been realized only very imperfectly. In fact, even though a large measure of agreement on general directions is always reached, resistance and opposition appear as soon as the moment comes for deriving the consequences, making choices, and, especially, paying the charges. The latter have been fixed at modest levels, well below the threshold of economic rationality. Nonetheless, it has been necessary to grant reductions and financial aids for the payments to be made by certain industries. Thus, the agencies have not really succeeded in regulating decisions and behavior. Even with a progressive increase of the charge rates, economic rationality cannot be the miraculous solution for the field of water management: it overlooks the residual irrationality of any kind of human behavior. The legislators of 1964 knew this, for they anticipated an extension of administrative

25. Freeman, Haveman, and Kneese, *The Economics of Environmental Pollution*, 170.
26. J. Picard, "Organization of Economic Water Management in France," cited in Johnson and Brown, *Cleaning up Europe's Waters*, 51.

powers and a reinforcement of the prevention and repression mechanism.[27]

Like the French, the Dutch approach to water pollution control relies primarily on a permit system and only secondarily on a charge system. In contrast to France, however, in the Netherlands serious efforts have been made to coordinate the two systems. Under the 1969 Surface Waters Purification Act, all water boards (waterschappen) and provinces that manage water quality must adopt effluent charges, to be operated in coordination with existing permit systems.

Officially, the sole purpose of effluent charges is the collection of the money needed to finance programs of pollution abatement. The process of charge setting differs between the regional and the national levels. Charges levied regionally by water boards tend to depend on the historic cost of treatment, so that the charge is low if the treatment plants were installed when construction costs were low. The charge on "national waters" is determined by a process of political bargaining between the Ministry of Economic Affairs, which favors relatively high charges, and the Ministry for Transport and Water Affairs, which has jurisdiction over the water boards and favors lower rates. Formally, the charge is set at a level that will recover 60 percent of the capital cost of removing the current pollution in national waters.[28]

Charges differ considerably across regional water boards, but the differences are based on regional and historical variations in the cost of building treatment plants, rather than on a recognition of the variability of environmental conditions. As in France, pollution coefficients are determined on an industry-wide basis, without taking firm-to-firm differences into account. Moreover, for small firms the charges are computed on the basis of the number of employees, the level of production, or the level of water consumption, rather than on actual effluent flows. For households and polluters that produce less than ten pollution

27. Fenet, "L'Administration de l'eau en France," 396.
28. Johnson and Brown, *Cleaning up Europe's Waters*, 88.

units, charges are set at a flat rate which does not vary with pollution loads. Thus, the system is not sensitive to variations in level of environmental damage, and this insensitivity will become even more pronounced if attempts to unify charges across water boards should succeed.

It has already been pointed out that Dutch charges, though not sufficient to cover the costs of water treatment fully, are significantly higher than in France. They have also been rising faster, in real as well as nominal terms. The basic reason for this difference is that while French charges are not indexed, Dutch fees, at least at the national level, are tied to the costs of building new treatment plants, and with inflation these costs have been rising dramatically.

The charges may even be high enough to provide incentives for innovation in pollution-abatement technology, but the use of industry-wide pollution coefficients tends, as in France, to limit this incentive effect. It is also necessary to emphasize that Dutch fees are not effluent charges in the sense in which environmental economists use the term, but rather taxes earmarked to finance the capital costs of pollution abatement. Hence, as a Dutch analyst points out, the effectiveness and legitimacy of the system are based not so much on environmental values as on the general liability to taxation. Firms that try to avoid paying the charges are regarded as tax-evaders.[29]

In Germany a nationwide system of effluent charges has been introduced only in 1981, under the 1976 law on waste water charges (Abwasserabgabengesetz). The charge was to be set initially at DM 20 per year per pollution unit (this corresponded to the estimated cost of service from secondary treatment facilities), but because of political opposition it was eventually set at DM 12. It has been increased to DM 40 in 1986.

It is too early to evaluate the German experience at the national level. At the regional level, however, charges have been used for a much longer time. For example, in the Ruhr region,

29. Hans Bressers, "The Role of Effluent Charges in Dutch Water Quality Policy," in Downing and Hanf, *International Comparisons in Implementing Pollution Laws*, 163.

one of the most heavily industrialized and densely populated areas in the world, charges were introduced in the years immediately preceding the First World War. The system developed in the Ruhr region has served as a model for the more recent developments in water management in France and the Netherlands. This explains a number of structural similarities among the three countries.

Water quality management in the Ruhr relies on a mixed system of permits and charges. Permits are issued by state (Land) authorities, while the charges are set by specialized associations or "cooperatives" (Wassergenossenschaften) whose compulsory membership includes all major polluter interests. As in France and the Netherlands, the permit system is the primary component: the permit, not payment of the charge, grants the right to pollute. The main purpose of the charges is to provide financial means to cover part of the costs of the pollution abatement programs defined by the associations. The charges can be kept fairly low since generous subsidies from the state cover up to 80 percent of total treatment costs, and almost half of the remaining costs are paid by nonpolluters.[30]

The method of setting charges is structurally similar to the methods already described for France and the Netherlands, although the specific formulas vary. Each firm in an industry is assumed to produce the same amount of waste per unit of production, unless it can prove otherwise. The charges are a function of production or water use, not of pollution directly, and do not vary with the location of firms. Thus, it is doubtful that the water quality goals of the Ruhr associations are achieved at least cost. The associations are highly efficient engineering organizations, but they do not ask economic questions about the net social benefits of their programs.[31] Charges are used to finance the programs, not to achieve a least-cost solution, let alone an optimal level of pollution.

For the purpose of the present discussion, the similarities of the various approaches are more significant than the differences

30. Johnson and Brown, *Cleaning up Europe's Waters*, 131.
31. Ibid., 130.

in technical details and administrative arrangements. The results of our survey may be summarized in the following propositions:

1. A pure charge system does not exist anywhere. What we observe are loose combinations of administrative, economic, and technical elements, in which traditional instruments (permits, licenses, standards) play the main role, charges only a secondary role.
2. Actual systems differ dramatically from theoretical models. In no country does the charge accurately reflect environmental damages; in fact, damages are not even estimated. The charge setters do not attempt to balance the incremental costs and the incremental benefits of further pollution abatement.
3. The incentive effect of the charges is seriously compromised by the generally low level of the fees, by the widespread use of subsidies, and by the fact that each firm in an industry is assumed to produce the same amount of waste per unit of output.
4. In all three countries charges amount to only a fraction of the total cost of pollution abatement. Despite official endorsement of the "polluter pays" principle, polluters can count on generous subsidies and other financial aids.
5. Finally, the empirical evidence shows that "nothing in the nature of a charge makes it immune to the political virus."[32] Bargains between charge setters and representatives of various polluter interests are ubiquitous, though they may take different forms in different countries. Even measurement procedures are negotiated in a political process whose outcomes reflect the relative power of polluters.[33]

THE CHOICE OF POLICY INSTRUMENTS

These conclusions are not intended to imply that charges, where they have been tried, have proved to be ineffective. Treatment capacity in France has increased dramatically since enactment of the 1964 law. Water quality in the Ruhr is remarkably high—though improvements in water quality have been achieved partly at the cost of air quality. In the Netherlands, a recent study shows, the organic pollution produced by fourteen industrial

32. Clifford Russell, "What Can We Get from Effluent Charges?", 270.
33. Johnson and Brown, *Cleaning up Europe's Waters*, 265.

branches was reduced by almost 79 percent between 1969, when charges were introduced, and 1980.[34]

The point is, rather, that such results do not prove that charges are superior to other policy instruments. First, substantial progress in pollution control has also been made in countries like Great Britain and Sweden that continue to rely primarily on a system of permits and effluent standards. Second, it is difficult to sort out the net effects of charges in the three countries considered because of the concomitant use of subsidies and other financial aids. Last but certainly not least, the charge approaches we have discussed differ so much from the pure system that it is impossible to derive any firm conclusion about the effectiveness, or even the feasibility, of such a system. About all one can say is that it is not obvious that *actual* charge systems are superior to *actual* systems of effluent standards.

Incidentally, such a cautious conclusion seems all the more appropriate in view of a recent survey indicating that even among economists the proportion of those who are convinced of the superiority of charges is much smaller than one would assume from the near unanimous endorsement by textbooks on environmental economics. According to this survey, which was conducted in 1979 among American economists and in 1981 among Austrian, French, German, and Swiss economists, only 31 percent agreed with the proposition that an effluent charge was superior to effluent standards (32 percent agreed with qualifications, and 37 percent disagreed). The breakdown by countries shows that support for effluent charges is particularly weak in Europe: only 19 percent of the Austrian economists surveyed, 21 percent of the Swiss, 27 percent of the French, and 36 percent of the Germans believed that charges were superior to standards, while 57 percent, 42 percent, 33 percent, and 43 percent, respectively, disagreed.[35]

Such differences in professional opinion are another indica-

34. Bressers, "The Role of Effluent Charges in Dutch Water Quality Management."

35. Bruno S. Frey, Friedrich Schneider, and Werner W. Pommerehne, "Effluent Taxes and Economists: A Love Affair?", *Zeitschrift für Umweltpolitik* 5, no. 2 (1983): 187–94.

tion of the inconclusiveness of both theoretical arguments and the empirical evidence. It seems that in choosing between charges and standards (and probably among policy instruments in general) people, including economists, are not primarily guided by narrow technical criteria like efficiency or effectiveness, but by broader policy preferences. Some economists who strongly endorse pollution charges, for example, admit at the same time that in the present state of knowledge one cannot predict the consequences of introducing any specific set of charges. What is important, in their opinion, is to establish the principle that environmental inputs should be priced; the problem of calculating the correct prices can be solved later.[36]

Of course, this amounts to considering effluent charges as policy targets rather than instruments. But if charges become an end in themselves, then questions of efficiency or effectiveness do not even arise. The basic question becomes: Are charges intrinsically so desirable that we should be willing to accept a charge that has been set with little knowledge of the likely environmental consequences and, for this very reason, open to intense political pressures?[37]

This value question cannot be settled by technical arguments. Those who believe that the extension of market principles to previously nonpriced things will increase the role of rationality in the ordering of human affairs are likely to give a positive answer. Conversely, many environmentalists and others who reject utilitarian principles in the realm of values would answer the question negatively. Philosophically, these two polar attitudes correspond to the distinction made in chapter 4 between an end-state maximizing, or utilitarian, position and a side-constraints, or Kantian, position. As noted there, a good utilitarian is prepared to sacrifice some of any value or goal to obtain more of other values or goals, while a Kantian treats moral values as binding constraints. To an environmentalist, environmental quality is a moral value and as such should not be traded off at

36. For a typical expression of this philosophy, see Kneese and Schultze, *Pollution, Prices, and Public Policy*, chap. 7.
37. Clifford Russell, "What Can We Get from Effluent Charges?", 260.

the margin; charges are a "license to pollute" because they allow such tradeoffs, while environmental standards are constraints imposed by society on morally unacceptable behavior.

One may question the logical consistency of this position—whenever values are in conflict, some tradeoff is unavoidable—but not its persuasive force in the forum of public deliberation. A survey conducted among staff members of Congress, environmental groups, and trade associations shows quite clearly that proposals to use economic incentives to control pollution tend to be evaluated in ideological or moral terms by supporters as well as opponents of effluent charges. Concerns about the kind of society in which we want to live were mentioned much more frequently than arguments about efficiency, effectiveness, or incentives to innovation.[38]

To repeat, the choice of policy instruments is not a technical problem that can be safely delegated to experts. It raises institutional, social, and moral issues that must be clarified through a process of public deliberation and resolved by political means. The naive faith of some analysts in the fail-safe properties of certain instruments allegedly capable of lifting the entire regulatory process out of the morass of political debate and compromise can only be explained by the constraining hold on their minds of a model of policy-making in which decisions are, in James Buchanan's words, "handed down from on high by omniscient beings who cannot err."[39]

In fact, neither theoretical arguments nor the available evidence prove conclusively the superiority of those instruments. What is more, actual regulatory systems differ so much from the systems discussed in textbooks that no reasonable inference from the data to the theoretical model is possible. We have also seen that major polluters generally succeed in keeping the level of effluent charges too low to achieve substantial efficiency gain. Thus, market approaches to regulation prove to be as subject to

38. Steven Kelman, *What Price Incentives?* (Boston: Auburn House, 1981).

39. "Toward Analysis of Closed Behavioral Systems," in J. M. Buchanan and R. D. Tollison, *Theory of Public Choice* (Ann Arbor: University of Michigan Press, 1972), 12.

political pressure and bargaining as the traditional administrative methods.

It is not surprising, therefore, that arguments about the theoretical properties of various instruments should play only a minor role in the policy debate. Experienced policy actors know that results depend upon institutional structures, so that the important choice is not among abstract methods but among specific institutional arrangements to implement them. Formal analysis at its best reveals the limits of what is theoretically achievable in public policy. In order to find out what can actually be achieved in a particular situation, analysts must also consider procedures and institutions—and people's attempts to manipulate them. To paraphrase Kant, policy analysis without institutional analysis is empty; institutional analysis without policy analysis is blind.

SEVEN

Policy Development

The relation of theories and arguments to policies and institutions, and the role of ideas in guiding policy development, are recurring themes of this book. In chapter 2, for example, I noted that President Roosevelt did not have to learn about government spending from Keynes. However, as Keynes's ideas came to dominate the thinking of economists and politicians, they helped to make expansionist fiscal policy the core idea of liberal economic policy for several decades. Again, in chapter 4 I argued that what is politically feasible within given constraints, and even the constraints themselves, depend on the limits of popular knowledge and the relationship between popularly accepted values and current policy. As Walter Heller put it, major policy breakthroughs are possible only after public opinion has been conditioned to accept new ideas and new concepts of the public interest.

To recall another example of the influence of ideas on policy development, in the 1950s the issue of poverty was a minor one in American public consciousness. In the 1960s, although the level and distribution of income had scarcely changed, it became a significant part of public policies. The new element was the emergence of an intellectual consensus about the "structural" causes of poverty.

If it is true, as this and other examples suggest, that objective conditions are seldom so compelling or so clear that they set the policy agenda or dictate a specific policy response, then it follows that an adequate account of policy development must take into account theories and ideas as much as technology and economics.

At the same time, one must be aware of the rationalist fallacy of believing that theories and ideas alone are powerful enough to determine the course of events, and of interpreting policy-making as a purely intellectual exercise (see chapters 1, 5, and 6). All important policies require political and moral choices to be made in a context that is characterized by norms, beliefs, goals, and pressures which differ from those of an academic community.[1]

Students of public policy have traditionally handled questions about the production and use of ideas as if these were abstract activities taking place in some sphere quite detached from the actual processes of policy-making. I have repeatedly argued that this separation is impossible. Conceptualizations, norms, and evaluative criteria emerge from and develop along with the practical and professional activities in which policymakers, administrators, judges, critics, and analysts are engaged. In the present chapter I will indicate ways in which the order of ideas and the order of events may be fitted together to provide a reasonably unified picture of policy development.

POLICY AND META-POLICY

The problem of fitting together ideas and events is not unique to policy analysis. Legal scholars face a similar problem when they analyze the development of the law. These scholars recognize that a legal system includes not only legal institutions, legal rules, and legal decisions, but also what lawmakers, judges,

---

1. Donald Winch, *Economics and Policy: A Historical Study* (New York: Walker, 1970), 18.

and legal scholars say about the law. Moreover, the relationship between legal theory and legal institutions is a dialectic one: the theory describes and evaluates those institutions, but at the same time those institutions, which would otherwise be disconnected and unorganized, become conceptualized and systematized, and thus transformed, by legal argument. As Harold J. Berman writes in *Law and Revolution*, the law contains within itself a legal science, a "meta-law," by which it can be both analyzed and evaluated.[2]

Thus, legal argument is viewed as a constituent activity of the legal process itself, and the development of legal institutions is not artificially separated from the development of theories about these institutions. As in the law, so in other professional activities, standards of arguments, evaluative criteria, professional goals, and rational ideals "emerge from, develop along with, and are refined in the light of the explanatory, practical, and/or judicial activities in which scientists, lawyers, and other 'rational craftsmen' are engaged."[3]

Extending this line of reasoning, there is a dialectic relationship between policy and "meta-policy"—the ideas, conceptualizations, and proposals advanced by policy actors, analysts, academics, and bureaucratic experts who share an active interest in that policy. Policy, as Hugh Heclo pointed out some years ago, is not a self-defining phenomenon. There is no unique set of decisions, actors, and institutions constituting policy and waiting to be discovered and described. Rather, policy is an intellectual construct, an analytic category the contents of which must first be identified by the analyst.[4] Hence, our understanding of a policy and its outcomes cannot be separated from the ideas, theories, and criteria by which the policy is analyzed and evaluated.

2. *Law and Revolution* (Cambridge: Harvard University Press, 1983), 8. See also Roberto Mangabeira Unger, *Knowledge and Politics* (New York: Free Press, 1975), esp. 106–19.

3. Stephen Toulmin, *Human Understanding* (Princeton, N.J.: Princeton University Press, 1972), 313.

4. "Review Article: Policy Analysis," *British Journal of Political Science* 2 (Jan. 1972):83–108.

Despite the insights of Heclo and a few other scholars, traditional conceptualizations of policy-making have failed to link the intellectual and political, economic and institutional aspects of the process by close ties of mutual relevance. This is true of the conceptualization of policy-making as planning or decision-making "writ large"—the technocratic model favored by analysts of the decisionist school—but also of the political model that views policy as the outcome of a power struggle, the resultant of conflicting interests and pressures.

The failure to link together ideas and events has seriously reduced the ability of these models to explain how policies change. The technocratic model explains policy change as the result of policymakers changing their preferences or adapting their goals to changes in objective (that is, economic or technological) conditions. But, as I noted above, objective conditions are seldom so compelling and unambiguous as to determine timing and direction of policy innovations. Moreover, not all policy development is planned; policies, as Henry Mintzberg observes, can form without necessarily being formulated.[5]

The political model of policy-making, on the other hand, explains policy development primarily as the result of changes in the configuration of dominant interests. Unplanned policy change is seen as the resultant of political, economic, and bureaucratic forces pulling in different directions. Such explanations, too, miss a great deal that is important for understanding policy development. As noted previously, the political and institutional development of policy is always accompanied by a parallel intellectual process of debate and argument. Participants marshal evidence in support of their proposals, use analysts and experts to challenge the assumptions of their opponents, and make arguments that appeal to the beliefs and values, as well as to the interests, of broader constituencies.

Also, there is empirical evidence that at least in some cases policy development is caused more by changes in beliefs and values than by changes in economic and political interests. Thus,

5. "Emergent Strategy for Public Policy," J. J. Carson Lecture Series, Faculty of Administration, University of Ottawa, 26 Sept. 1985.

according to James Q. Wilson, "only by the most extraordinary theoretical contortions can one explain the Auto Safety Act, the 1964 Civil Rights Act, the OSH Act, or most environmental protection laws by reference to the economic stakes involved."[6] Similarly, in none of the cases of deregulation analyzed by Martha Derthick and Paul Quirk did the regulated industries decide that regulation was no longer in their interest; nor was the defeat of the regulated industries brought about primarily by other well-organized groups that stood to gain from reform. Instead, these authors argue that the regulatory reforms of the late 1970s and early 1980s would never have occurred without the sustained intellectual critique of previous regulatory policies developed by economists in the preceding decade.[7]

Recent case studies by John S. Odell and Nelson W. Polsby provide other examples where intellectual factors have to be taken into consideration in order to explain the direction of new policy.[8] But even when policy change is best explained by the political and economic power of groups seeking selfish ends, those who attempt to justify those changes must appeal to the merits of particular issues. Legislators, administrators, analysts, critics, and the public at large wish to know whether the change is justified. All of them seek standards against which to judge the success of a policy and the merits of specific programs initiated within the framework of that policy.[9] Even policies that appear to have no conscious intellectual basis may nonetheless contain an implicit rationale which it is important to distill. In fact, changes in a policy or in its environment often lead to previously unnoticed or unexamined assumptions being noticed and examined.

6. "The Politics of Regulation," in J. Q. Wilson, ed., *The Politics of Regulation* (New York: Basic Books, 1980), 372.

7. Martha Derthick and Paul J. Quirk, *The Politics of Deregulation* (Washington, D.C.: Brookings Institution, 1985), 238–46.

8. John S. Odell, *U.S. International Monetary Policy* (Princeton, N.J.: Princeton University Press, 1982); Nelson W. Polsby, *Political Innovation in America* (New Haven: Yale University Press, 1984).

9. Stephen Breyer, *Regulation and Its Reform* (Cambridge: Harvard University Press, 1982), 10.

CORE AND PERIPHERY

Change may reveal not only unexamined assumptions, but also the underlying continuity of the policy framework. Like organizations, policies are constantly changing, but the most immediate experience of policy, for both actors and observers, is a sense of continuity through time. Continuity is equally important for the analyst, for without some stability and consistency in actions and expectations it would be impossible to detect any pattern in a stream of apparently disconnected decisions and discrete pieces of legislation and administration.

In short, both continuity and change are inherent in our conception of policy. What gives a policy stability is that some of its values, assumptions, methods, goals, and programs are held to be central and only to be abandoned, if at all, under the greatest stress and at the risk of severe internal crises. What gives the policy adaptability is that many values, assumptions, methods, goals, and programs are disposable, modifiable, or replaceable by new ones.

An analytic distinction is needed, therefore, between the relatively stable and rigid part of a policy and its more changing and flexible components. Using a visual metaphor, the stable part may be called the _core_ of the policy, the flexible part, its _periphery_. To say that the core represents the rigid part of the policy is not to suggest that it is immutable, but only that it changes more gradually and continuously than the elements of the periphery that are its transitory end-products. A radical transformation or abandonment of the core signifies a major change in policy—revolution rather than evolution, so to speak.

Especially important among the elements of the policy core are methods or strategies for translating general principles into concrete activities. Such strategies can be of two types, positive and negative. Positive strategies suggest or mandate permissible approaches or courses of action, while negative strategies discourage or prohibit other approaches or courses of action.

We may note in passing an interesting similarity between our notion of negative strategy and that of non–decision making introduced by Bachrach and Baratz. According to these authors, non–decision making is a method used by policymakers in order to block challenges to the prevailing allocation of values and choices, or to suppress new demands or incipient issues.[10] Now it may be true, as the critics argue, that a non-decision is a nonevent and thus not susceptible to empirical study. However, the concept could be made operational by translating the language of non–decision making into that of positive and negative strategies. Unlike a nonevent, a strategy, positive or negative, can be tracked empirically—for instance, through longitudinal research or by analyzing documentary evidence such as laws, regulations, official records, and public debate. Illustrations will be provided in the next section.

If the core provides continuity, the periphery—largely composed of programs and other concrete administrative activities that are intended to give effect to the core principles—provides flexibility. The need to adapt the particular programs through which the policy operates to ever-changing economic, social, and political conditions keeps the periphery in constant flux, but peripheral changes do not usually affect the core, except perhaps through their cumulative impact.

Thus, the distinction between core and periphery articulates the intuitive notion that not all policy changes are equally significant, nor all programs equally important. The closer some particular activity is to the core, the greater the pull to retain it and the sense of discontinuity when it is abandoned. For this reason it may be more useful to picture the policy core as being surrounded not by a single periphery but by several peripheries or, to use the language of the philosopher of science Imre Lakatos, "protective belts" arranged in concentric circles around the core.[11]

To speak of protective belts is to call attention to an important but often overlooked function of administrative programs and institutional arrangements. If the core is to provide continuity

10. Peter Bachrach and Morton Baratz, "Two Faces of Power," *American Political Science Review* 56 (Dec. 1962): 947–52. See also Bachrach and Elihu Bergman, *Power and Choice* (Lexington, Mass.: Lexington Books, 1983).

11. Imre Lakatos, "Criticism and the Methodology of Scientific Research Programmes," *Proceedings of the Aristotelian Society* 69 (1968): 149–86.

and a minimum of consistency in policy-making, it must be protected as much as possible from too frequent or far-reaching changes. Bipartisan foreign policy, for example, is an agreement among key policy actors to make certain core principles provisionally irrefutable, so to speak. Hence, debate, criticism, and reform must be redirected to the particular programs and activities that give effect to the core principles. In this sense, the various elements of the periphery form a protection around the core, deflecting criticism from basic principles as much as implementing them.

The model of a policy core surrounded by concentric peripheries (or protective belts) sheds some light on incrementalism as a method or style of policy-making. In our teminology, incremental changes are peripheral changes. The fact that most changes occur in the periphery explains why incrementalism is such a pervasive feature of policy-making. However, not all incremental changes of a given "size" are equally important. Rather, their importance depends on their distance from the policy core. As was noted above, the closer a proposed change is to the core, the stronger will be the resistance to it and the greater the policy consequences if it is accepted.

On the other hand, sharply defined core principles may facilitate, rather than inhibit, incremental change and adaptation to new situations by providing clear criteria by which to distinguish the essential from the expendable, and by setting up guidelines within which a wide variety of approaches can develop. Conversely, policies based on poorly articulated or ill-understood principles tend to become rigid and to discourage experimentation for fear of exposing the ambiguities that made the initial consensus possible. Hence, articulation and clarification of the policy core—an important task of retrospective analysis—can help experimentation and learning.

For the analyst it is as much of a problem to identify the relatively stable components of a policy as it is to understand how particular programs change. Even policy actors can seldom give a full list of their values, goals, methods, and assumptions, let alone separate them into core and periphery. Moreover, many of the goals and assumptions that an outside observer might think were implicit in the policy may never have been perceived or consciously articulated by the actors.

These difficulties remind us that policy is an analytic category constructed by the analyst rather than a directly observable phenomenon. Any rational reconstruction of human affairs is open to a number of potential pitfalls—hindsight, bias, oversimplification. But this is not to say that a clever analyst can transform any collection of pieces of legislation and administration into a policy, any more than the historian is free to discover in past events the unfolding of his preferred philosophy. There is, first, documentary evidence (legislative debates, laws, judicial decisions, official histories and records, and so on) against which the proposed reconstruction may be tested.

Second, the operational significance of positive and negative strategies should be evident in programmatic doctrines, standard operating procedures, preferred policy instruments, and rejected alternatives or non-decisions. Another important source of insight are the views and actions of both supporters and opponents of a given policy. Actors do not usually support or oppose with equal vigor all proposed changes in existing policy. Members of the coalition built around the core may not be seriously concerned with particular peripheral programs, while beneficiaries of these same programs are not necessarily committed to the policy core. These differentiated reactions can provide important clues about the relative centrality of the various structural elements of the policy.

It is also important to recognize when a set of political and administrative activities fails to qualify as a full-fledged policy. Two extreme cases may be mentioned here. In one case, the programs and decisions that the analyst observes are only the scattered remains of what was once a full-fledged policy—fragments of a protective structure that has turned into an empty shell. A policy core that is no longer able to produce new interesting ideas, that continues to fight yesterday's battles instead of attacking today's problems, may eventually lose political support and intellectual credibility. The core will atrophy until it is eventually replaced, but parts of the periphery may continue to exist for some time. Recent developments in economic policy exemplify the process of progressive decline of a policy core—orthodox Keynesianism—and, at the same time, the difficulty of reaching a new consensus. The failure of conservatives to institutionalize a radical-right revolution in economic policy and the obvious inadequacy of traditional liberal approaches reveal the vacuum that exists today in this crucial area of public policy.[12]

The second case in which it may be confidently asserted that no recognizable policy exists is when either a core has not yet emerged (this seems to be the case of the energy "policy" of many countries today) or some of its essential elements are missing. For example, in the early 1940s Walter Lippmann argued that for nearly fifty years the United States had not possessed "a settled and generally accepted foreign policy."[13] His argument, in the terminology of this chapter, is that in the period between the turn of the century and the early 1940s, the core of U.S. foreign policy was incomplete. It did include some general principles and far-reaching commitments—within the continental limits of the United States, in the Western Hemisphere, in the Pacific—but no instruments and credible strategies for giving effect to those principles and commitments.

ILLUSTRATIONS

The development of social security policy in the United States will serve as our first illustration of the concepts introduced in the preceding section. One of the most striking features of this development is that although the system has undergone constant incremental change since its creation in 1935, the changes have followed paths well defined by programmatic doctrines. From the very beginning the top management was quite clear about first principles: the program should be contributory, "universal," and compulsory; it should be national in scope and should be run by the federal government; benefits should be related to

12. Herbert Stein, *Presidential Economics* (New York: Simon and Schuster, 1984), 321–22.
13. *U.S. Foreign Policy: Shield of the Republic* (Boston: Little, Brown, 1943), 3.

wages; and having paid their contributions, insureds or their dependents should get benefits as a matter of right. These may be taken to be the core principles of social security policy.

The main positive strategy emphasizes the method of social insurance as the preferred technique of policy-making. According to this principle, not only is participation compulsory, but benefits are prescribed by law, rather than by contract, and the system is supposed to be mildly redistributive (in favor of insureds with many dependents and of participants who were elderly when the system was initiated). This strategy has been quite effective. As was mentioned in chapter 6, the prevailing technique of policy analysis in the Social Security Administration in the 1950s and 1960s was to identify a social problem, such as lack of health care, and to develop arguments and methods for dealing with it through social insurance.[14]

Not surprisingly, the main negative strategy rejects the principle of private insurance (according to which protection is voluntary and provided by many insurers in competition with each other, while the cost of each protection is determined on a strictly actuarial basis), but also opposes public assistance, means tests, and other "welfare" approaches to social problems.

The periphery of the social security policy contains many elements. However, program executives and key political supporters do not consider all programmatic elements equally important, that is, equally close to the core. Old Age and Survivors Insurance (OASI), for example, is much more central, and hence more carefully protected, than, say, Old Age Assistance (OAA). In a metric that measures distance from the core, Disability Insurance and Medicare occupy an intermediate position between OASI and OAA, being closer to the former than to the latter program.

Thus, social security policy in the United States (as in most European countries) has a recognizable core containing a sharply defined set of principles and methodological rules. At the same time, however, this core allows a considerable amount of choice

14. Martha Derthick, *Policymaking for Social Security* (Washington, D.C.: Brookings Institution, 1979).

in operations. The program does not have to be financed only by contributions, nor do people need to contribute very much for very long in order to qualify for benefits. Benefits should be related to wages, but the exact nature of the relationship may be determined in several different ways. Even the use of general revenues would be compatible with core principles, and has in fact been proposed very early by program executives.[15] In short, the periphery of the policy has proved to be remarkably flexible, and this flexibility has greatly contributed to the political success of the program.

British health policy under the National Health Service provides another instructive example. Created in 1946, the service has undergone a number of administrative and organizational changes but has preserved its basic commitment to the core principle that medical services should be distributed according to need rather than ability to pay. Its main positive strategy prescribes financial and administrative methods that are compatible with the basic principle (financing through general taxation, nationalization of private hospitals, and so on), while the negative strategy rules out other approaches such as user charges (with the exception of a few nonessential health services). Even proposals concerning "health vouchers" have so far been rejected, by Conservative as well as by Labour governments, as being incompatible with the principle of collective choice in health matters.

Problems of excessive demand created by the abolition of financial barriers have been tackled not by reintroducing price mechanisms (fees for services) but by setting budgetary limits on total health expenditures, administrative controls and improvements in hospital efficiency, and other peripheral adjustments. In fact, debate about the core, as opposed to particular aspects, of the National Health Service has been generally considered to be irrelevant. The following comments by Mark Blaug make the point quite clearly:

> Whether we like it or not, the British National Health Service effectively replaced individual choice in the distribution of health

15. Ibid., 21–23.

services by collective choice. Thus, arguments about "market failure" in justifying either government ownership or government finance are totally irrelevant in Britain, unless of course the thesis is that they ought to be made relevant by returning health to the market mechanism. It would seem that there is now a consensus among all segments of British society and among all shades of public opinion that health should be distributed in accordance with ability to pay, in other words, "communism in health."[16]

Neither Blaug nor any other competent analyst would deny that there are serious problems of allocation within the National Health Service. But as long as the consensus about the use of collective-choice mechanisms survives, solutions have to be found at the level of organization and management, without compromising the integrity of the policy core. The negative strategy of the system prohibits a return to the principle of ability-to-pay (for example, through generalized user charges), whatever the merits of such a move in terms of allocative efficiency.

To be sure, national health services and social security systems are unique in their size and scope, as well as in the explicitness of their ideological commitments. These features favor the articulation of comprehensive programmatic doctrines and thus facilitate the distinction between core principles and tactical adjustments. But every settled policy will exhibit a similar, if less clearly defined, structure. As I pointed out above, policymakers, when pressed for the exact statement of the principles guiding their actions, are often at a loss. This, however, is a common state of affairs with all kinds of principles. Craftsmen, businessmen, and athletes often know what to do in a certain situation without being able to state in words the principles on which they act. This does not mean that their actions do not proceed according to principles. The same is true of policymakers. Their inability or reluctance to spell out basic norms and commitments is no proof that their policies lack a more or less well-defined core.

16. *An Introduction to the Economics of Education* (Harmondsworth, England: Penguin, 1970), 324.

THE POLICY SPACE

The analytic categories developed so far describe the fine structure of a policy by decomposing it into core and periphery and then further subdividing these elements into various components. Policies can also be categorized by generic structural characteristics such as degree of fragmentation, maturity, or complexity. For example, the existence of different modes of transportation and of energy production and consumption implies that transportation and energy policies are more fragmented than, say, agricultural or health policy. Social security is more mature than environmental policy. These two policies differ also in degree of complexity: the latter attempts to change the behavior of millions of individuals, communities, and firms, while the main task of the former is collecting contributions and mailing monthly checks.

Many other categorizations are possible (for example, by issue or purpose), but even the most detailed description of internal structure and function may fail to reveal important interconnections across policy areas. It is a truism in policy-making that everything is related to everything else. Economic policy is closely linked to social policy, trade policy to foreign policy, environmental policy to industrial policy. Increasing policy interdependence has led to a proliferation of hybrid labels like "foreign economic policy" and even "intermestic policy"—meaning a policy that is predominantly domestic but has a significant impact abroad, or a policy that is primarily viewed by policymakers as foreign policy but has a significant domestic impact.[17]

It is practically impossible today to study policy development in isolation. This is not to say that one should or could take all interrelations into account: clearly, some linkages and intersections are more relevant to a particular policy than others. We introduce the term *policy space* to denote a set of policies that are so closely interrelated that it is not possible to make useful de-

17. Robert A. Pastor, *Congress and the Politics of U.S. Foreign Economic Policy* (Berkeley: University of California Press, 1980), 9.

scriptions of or analytic statements about one of them without taking the other elements of the set into account. "Space" is used here in the mathematical sense of a structured set of elements, as in "Euclidean space." The structure of a policy space includes both the internal arrangements of its elements and the linkages and intersections among them. In this terminology, "foreign policy," "domestic policy," or "social policy" are policy spaces rather than discrete policies or unstructured aggregates of pieces of legislation and administration.

Inherent in the notion of a policy space is a certain autonomy with respect both to the external environment (the "problem space") and to the plans and decisions of the policymakers (the "actor space"). As Aaron Wildavsky writes, all that has happened within a policy space determines most of what will happen in that space. Increasingly, policy becomes its own cause.[18]

The main reason for the growing autonomy of the policy space is ecological. As the population of policies grows relative to the size of the space, individual policies necessarily become more interdependent. The consequences produced by one policy are increasingly likely to interfere with the working of other policies. External diseconomies of many sorts, all of which may be summarized under the single term "congestion," clearly become more important as the number of policies, or their size and complexity, increase. Hence, new programs and institutional arrangements to prevent or reduce the consequences of congestion become necessary.

But in an already crowded policy space, solutions beget new problems in the form of policy overlaps, jurisdictional conflicts, and unanticipated consequences. Also, policy complexity tends to generate more complexity. For example, regulatory complexity creates the need for "rule intermediaries"—people like lawyers and accountants who specialize in the interpretation of ambiguous or conflicting rules. These specialists have a vested interest in resisting simplification of regulations. Thus, red tape

18. "Policy as Its Own Cause," in *Speaking Truth to Power* (Boston: Little, Brown, 1979), 62–85.

may not be simply the bureaucratic way of doing things, but also the more or less unintended result of rule complexity.[19]

One of the most striking manifestations of the autonomy of the policy space is the phenomenon of unplanned policy change. One important source of unplanned change is complexity of implementation. When a large measure of discretion is necessary to accomplish a certain task, implementation cannot be fully controlled. For instance, "street level bureaucrats" like teachers, judges, policemen, and social workers have considerable discretion in determining the nature, amount, and quality of the benefits and sanctions provided by their agencies. Their position permits them to decide more or less autonomously with respect to important aspects of their interactions with citizens. When taken together, their actions and decisions may add up to agency policy—but policy that no one has deliberately planned.[20]

Similarly, when in a new, difficult situation policymakers at the top lack the knowledge to establish a viable explicit policy, an unplanned policy can slowly emerge as different approaches are tried at lower levels and successful variants adopted by a variety of actors responding flexibly to local problems.[21] When discussing the policy/administration dichotomy in chapter 2, I noted that policies are initiated at all levels of an organization or policy-making body, not just at the top. As the present discussion suggests, this may be a particularly common phenomenon in a crowded policy space where implementation problems are compounded by interdependencies and policy overlaps.

In sum, a good deal of policy development is better explained as the result of processes originating in the policy space itself than as a response to changes in the external environment or in the configuration of economic and political interests. The autonomy of the policy space is the analytic expression of the fact that an increasingly significant part of the growth in public policy

19. J. R. Kearl, "Rules, Rule Intermediaries and the Complexity and Stability of Regulation," *Journal of Public Economics* 22 (1983): 215–26.

20. Michael Lipsky, *Street-Level Bureaucracy* (New York: Russell Sage Foundation, 1980).

21. Mintzberg, *Emergent Strategy for Public Policy*, 8.

is the consequence, often unanticipated, of previous policies and their interconnections and overlaps.

CONCEPTUAL INNOVATION AND POLICY DEVELOPMENT

The capacity of policymakers to respond to incessant change in economic conditions, political climate, and societal values, despite the growing autonomy of the policy space, depends crucially on the availability of a rich pool of ideas and proposals. The existing stock of ideas shapes their response to events by defining the conceptual alternatives from among which they choose. On what conditions will the production of new ideas be intense or slow, or more intense in one policy area than in another? Why are some proposals accepted while others are rejected or ignored? How is conceptual innovation linked to policy development?

To pose such questions is to suggest that policy development may be analyzed as the outcome of a dual process of conceptual innovation and of selection by political actors from the pool of available policy variants. The locus of conceptual innovation will be called the *policy community*, while the political arena is the locus of selection.

A policy community is composed of specialists who share an active interest in a certain policy or set of related policies: academics, professionals, analysts, policy planners, media, and interest-group experts. The members of a policy community represent different interests, hold different values, and may be engaged in different research programs, but they all contribute to policy development by generating and debating new ideas and proposals.

Although some members of a policy community may also be political actors, the two roles are distinct. A voter choosing in a referendum or a policymaker choosing among different options does not contribute to conceptual innovation; rather, he acts as a mechanism for selecting from the pool of available variants. The whole political process, in fact, may be thought of as a large selection mechanism that picks out for acceptance those of the competing policy ideas which in some sense best meet the demands of the political environment.

The effectiveness of the selection procedures will depend on the rate and quality of conceptual innovation. Without a continuous stream of new proposals selection will have nothing to work on. In turn, conceptual innovation depends on political and institutional factors as well as on the research agenda of the members of a policy community. For example, until recently expert critics of social security in the United States and in Europe lacked a disciplinary and organizational base through which access to the relevant political arena could be secured. As Martha Derthick's *Policymaking for Social Security* shows, the actuarial profession in the United States had produced some penetrating analyses of the problems of social security in the late 1930s, but critical discussion occurred infrequently after the founding period. Actuarial conventions in general ceased to pay much attention to the subject.

On the other hand, American economists began developing a substantial amount of fundamental analyses of social security only in the 1960s. Economists writing on social security before that date either were outside the mainstream of their discipline or their interest was really directed at different, broader issues— Keynesian economists, for instance, who thought of social security primarily as an instrument of fiscal policy. Social security executives and their supporters in Congress could easily disregard criticisms from individual experts who lacked widespread professional support.[22] All this has changed with the recurrent financial crises of recent years. These crises, and a changing climate of opinion about the proper role of government in the economy, have stimulated a much more sustained intellectual effort by economists and other analysts to develop more or less radical proposals to reform the present system.

As this example shows, lack of access to the appropriate forum may, by itself, be a serious obstacle to the proper consideration of new policy ideas. Systematic development and evaluation of

22. Derthick, *Policymaking for Social Security*.

new proposals is impossible without organized opportunities for critical debate. The policy community must be sufficiently open and competitive so that truly novel variants may emerge. The use by government agencies of outside sources of knowledge, advice, and evaluation is one way of increasing the flow of conceptual innovations. At the same time, selection can be effective only where the community is not *too* open. If each and every proposal were taken seriously, the burden for the selection mechanisms would soon become unbearable, leading to a breakdown of evaluative criteria. A distinguishing feature of a well-functioning intellectual community is that every argument presented must relate to some point of view already present in the community. A new proposal will be judged not by its intellectual merits alone, but by inquiring how it might contribute to the ongoing debate.[23] Hence, only some of the theoretically conceivable proposals and policy variants can become active topics of debate and innovation at any given time. Neither a national health service nor nationalized railroads, for instance, are significant topics of debate in the United States, even among policy experts. The dominant ideology of free enterprise and limited government inhibits serious consideration of such topics, just as in the welfare states of Western Europe the consensus that health care should be distributed according to need rather than ability to pay inhibits serious consideration of proposals to return health care to market mechanisms. Thus, the influence of the policy core in determining which proposals and critical arguments are taken seriously and which are considered irrelevant in policy terms, extends also to the debate within the policy community.

It should be noted, however, that policy experts have their own research agenda which reflects disciplinary or professional concerns rather than political events like elections and changes of administration. Hence, while many ideas are discarded because the experts cannot conceive of any plausible circumstances under which they could find political support, some intellectually interesting ideas are kept alive, despite pessimism about their

23. Unger, *Knowledge and Politics*, 110–16.

short-term political feasibility, in the hope that the larger political climate will change.[24] Academic criticism of government regulation of competitive industries is an example. To a remarkable extent, American economists agreed on the inefficiency of regulation long before deregulation began to be instituted in industries like airlines, trucking, and telecommunications.

According to a widespread view of knowledge utilization in policy-making, research provides the knowledge and information needed to solve a problem; policymakers then reach a solution. The evolutionary model of conceptual innovation and political selection sketched above suggests that knowledge plays a more indirect role. Political actors select their ideas and arguments from the supply that happens to be available at a given time, and these are usually the results of intellectual efforts of preceding years. As Derthick and Quirk write, events occur too fast and ideas mature too slowly for responses to be devised anew for each pressing situation.[25]

The absence of a direct causal relationship between knowledge and policy is also due to the loose-jointed structure of policy communities. Because the different members of a policy community have their own professional, intellectual, and ideological commitments, ideas seldom preserve their original form in the process of diffusion through debate and argument. New meanings and interpretations emerge at each stage, leading to new formulations of the underlying issues. Thus, the "energy problem" of the 1970s, originally formulated as the problem of ensuring cheap and abundant energy for continued economic growth, was soon modified to include issues like energy conservation, economic growth versus environmental quality, the hazards of plutonium production and the danger of nuclear proliferation, geopolitics and national independence, and the relative advantages of centralized and decentralized modes of energy production.

Instead of producing single, well-defined solutions, the policy

---

24. John W. Kingdon, *Agendas, Alternatives, and Public Policies* (Boston: Little, Brown, 1984), 140–45.

25. *The Politics of Deregulation,* 57.

debate leads to a sequence of issue transformations and to a corresponding expansion of the boundary of the policy community. The creation of stable coalitions around a particular conceptualization of the problem under discussion is the task of political actors, not of policy intellectuals.

It should also be noted that our evolutionary model of variation and selection in no way implies that the theoretically most interesting idea always, or even usually, carries the day. As the failure of the advocates of effluent charges in the United States shows, a policy idea will not be adopted unless it is communicated persuasively and meets the demands of the political environment. Economic arguments against government regulation of essentially competitive markets met these criteria. They were persuasive because they were supported by a consensus of professional opinion and by the prevailing ideology of market competition, and because the first results of deregulation in the airline industry seemed to confirm theoretical predictions about benefits to the consumers. Moreover, proposals for economic deregulation could be linked persuasively to broader public concerns—inflation, big government, and consumer protection.

For key political actors the idea of regulatory reform became a convenient and effective way of addressing such public concerns. In turn, political sponsorship gave added force to an idea that seemed to be well suited to the needs of different groups of policy actors. To quote again Derthick and Quirk, "Finally, deregulation—by this time often vaguely defined and loosely applied—became a preferred style of policy choice in the nation's capital, espoused more or less automatically, even unthinkingly, by a wide range of office holders and their critics and used by them as a guide to position taking."[26] As these authors argue, what ultimately made the idea of deregulation relevant to politics were less the theoretical elaborations of it than events that no one, including the original academic proponents, could have foreseen: the development of severe inflation, the rise of consumerism, and a widely diffused disaffection with big government.

26. Ibid., 35.

The main thesis of this chapter is that an adequate theory of policy development requires that attention be paid to ideas, theories, and arguments as well as to technology, economics, and politics. Analysis and arguments conceptualize, and thus transform, the institutions and processes of policy-making. At the same time, institutional and political factors influence the rate and quality of conceptual innovation and determine which among the available proposals will be selected for actual use. Thus, the relationship between policy and its intellectual superstructure, or meta-policy, is a dialectic one.

For the student of policy development it is as much of a problem to explain the continuity of the policy framework as it is to explain how particular programs and institutional arrangements change within that framework. The distinction between core and periphery has been introduced with this particular problem in mind.

An adequate theory of policy development must also take into consideration that an increasingly significant part of the growth of public policy is the consequence of previous policies and their interconnections and overlaps, rather than the result of deliberate choice. The emergence of unplanned policies is too important a phenomenon to be dismissed as the random resultant of political, economic, or bureaucratic forces pulling in different directions. In many cases, unplanned change is best explained in terms of endogenous processes taking place in a relatively autonomous policy space.

Finally, the link between conceptual and policy development is provided by an evolutionary model according to which changes in current policy may be analyzed as the outcome of a dual process of conceptual variation and subsequent selection from the pool of available policy variants. The policy community is the locus of conceptual innovation, while the political arena is the locus of selection. The dialectic relationship between policy and meta-policy finds concrete expression in the interactions between a policy community and the corresponding political arena.

EIGHT

Evaluation and Accountability

The debate through which criteria of evaluation and standards of accountability are established is an essential part of the process of policy development. In fact, the dialogue among legislators, policymakers, and the electorate whereby policy is formed in a system of government by discussion is always, directly or indirectly, about evaluative issues. Analysts have contributed to this debate in a number of ways, but especially through the new subdiscipline of evaluation research.

Evaluation research is a large and expanding area of policy analysis devoted to collecting, testing, and interpreting information about the implementation and effectiveness of existing policies and public programs. As I noted in a previous chapter, the importance achieved by evaluation research within the field of professional policy analysis shows that analysts have finally come to realize that the effective delivery of public services requires more than the design of some theoretically optimal program. Even more important is to learn how the program is actually implemented, who benefits and who loses from it, whether the program is accomplishing what was intended, and if not, how it can be improved or discontinued.

Many evaluators seem to assume that these are purely empirical determinations, involving neither value choices nor personal opinions. In fact, values and opinions count a great deal in evaluation not only because of the ambiguity of the outcomes of practice—the difficulty of assigning specific causes to particular effects, of measuring outputs, and assessing unintended consequences, of distinguishing between flawed conceptions and failures of implementation—but even more because of inescapable disagreements about the kind of evaluative criteria that are meaningful, fair, or politically acceptable in a given situation. Such ambiguities and disagreements can never be fully resolved by improved measurement and testing techniques, but can be represented and clarified by debate and mutual persuasion. In order to understand the role of argument in evaluation it is essential to distinguish between standard setting and standard using.

In chapter 2 I drew a parallel distinction between norm setting and norm using—between defining the criteria of what constitutes a policy problem and searching for solutions that satisfy those criteria. The distinction between setting and using standards is equally important in evaluation. At the standard-setting stage, or when a reform of evaluative standards is being considered, it is open to anyone to put forward a proposal as to what the standards should be and to use persuasion in order to influence others to accept the proposal. Objective analysis—for instance, to clarify the consequences of adopting a particular set of criteria, or to point out logical inconsistencies among different standards—can provide useful inputs to the debate, but cannot play a decisive role at this stage. Empirical determinations that show whether certain standards are in fact attained become relevant only after agreement about the appropriate evaluative standards is reached. Because reaching agreement on standards is so difficult in the presence of different values and interests, much evaluation analysis is really concerned with the merits of various standard-setting proposals rather than with the application of particular standards of merit to a given program.

MULTIPLE EVALUATION

Professional evaluation is only a small part of the general process of criticism and appraisal of public policies to which all politically active members of a democratic community contribute in different but equally useful ways. Arguments about standard-setting proposals play an even bigger role in policy criticism than in professional program evaluation. Policies and policy instruments are constantly assessed, ex ante and ex post, from the diverse critical perspectives of legislators, judges, policymakers, program managers, implementing bureaucrats, interest groups, independent experts, the media, and private citizens.

These perspectives are different both because evaluative criteria vary with the role and position of the evaluator and because different evaluators tend to focus their attention on different aspects of the policy-making process. General standards of performance like legality, legitimacy, economy, effectiveness, efficiency, or responsiveness to public needs are characteristically related to the distinct roles of judges, politicians, budget officers, public accountants, and consumers of public services or their political representatives. Moreover, some criteria, such as efficiency and effectiveness, apply primarily to the outputs or outcomes of public policy, other criteria (for instance, economy) apply to the inputs, and others still (legality, legitimacy) to the process that transforms inputs into outputs.

This multiplicity of evaluative standards and critical perspectives reflects the complexity of policy-making in a pluralistic society. Experience shows that debate among advocates of different criteria is often useful in reaching agreement and permits a more sophisticated understanding of public policy than is possible from a single perspective. Even professional evaluators now recognize that their work becomes relevant only in the broader context of competing criteria and evidence presented by various actors and interest groups. The new slogan is "multiple evaluation." This phrase acknowledges the legitimacy of different criteria and perspectives, but also suggests the need to reach a level of understanding that is more than the sum of the separate evaluations. As I said earlier, the purpose of multiple evaluation is not to combine all the partial criteria into one general criterion of good policy, but to contribute to a shared understanding of the various critical perspectives and of their different functions in the process of public deliberation.

Multiple evaluation starts with two basic questions: "Evaluation by whom?" and "Evaluation of what?" The first question emphasizes the importance of accounting for the presence of different evaluative *roles*, while the second question directs our attention to the three basic *modes* of evaluation—inputs evaluation, outcomes evaluation, and process evaluation.

EVALUATIVE ROLES

Policy or program evaluation serves a wide variety of uses and users. That different criteria are used by people in different roles is not a bad thing as such. It simply reflects the various needs, interests, and concerns of different actors and stakeholders. So long as the judgments expressed from the perspective of one particular role are not presented or misinterpreted as judgments relevant to or speaking for all possible roles, we have a healthy state of multiple or pluralistic evaluation.

Difficulties begin to arise when this neat partitioning of roles and the criticism voiced from them is not possible. Unfortunately, such breakdowns seem to be more the rule than the exception in practice. Perhaps the most common problem occurs when the conclusions of an evaluation done for use in a particular role are assumed to be equally relevant from the perspective of other roles with different evaluative criteria. Because roles and criteria are mismatched, the conclusions of the evaluation are almost inevitably found wanting.

Such difficulties arise, for example, when academic ecologists are convened as the sole reviewers of the environmental impact assessment mandated in the United States for federal projects. From the perspective of a project manager or administrative law judge, the relevant evaluative criteria might be the timeliness of the assessment, the likelihood that potentially serious impacts have been noted, and, perhaps, whether practical development alternatives are suggested. From the ecologists' point of view, however, such criteria are at best vaguely comprehended and given only secondary consideration. Their evaluation would likely be based on such criteria as the adequacy of sampling design, the use of appropriate theory, and the accurate characterization and quantification of uncertainties. As a result, the ecologists may accept or reject attempted impact assessments for reasons that are largely irrelevant to the people who will eventually have to resolve the practical problems of environmental management.[1]

Examples of mismatched criteria abound in professional evaluations of public programs. Many program evaluations have a narrow managerial focus, being concerned with goal achievement and administrative control rather than with the responsiveness of the program to the divergent values of different individuals and groups. Such a narrow perspective neglects a more structural analysis of changes in societal values and of the ability of bureaucracy to adapt to such changes. This may be the most important information from the point of view of top policymakers.

In turn, bureaucrats often feel that the stress placed by many evaluation studies on effectiveness and efficiency is in conflict with such basic values as employee participation, personal development, and high morale. Others question how economic rationality should be balanced against professional standards. Again, evaluation done to learn about a program's operations and its effects—information that is important for allocating resources and drafting new guidelines—may be unsatisfactory as a means of controlling the implementing agency.

Is there a cure for such common tendencies to confound evaluative roles or to mismatch criteria? Probably not. At a minimum, however, efforts to build a critical capacity for judging particular programs or entire policies should explicitly recognize that multiple roles exist, each with a legitimate claim to set eval-

1. William C. Clark and Giandomenico Majone, "The Critical Appraisal of Scientific Inquiries with Policy Implications," *Science, Technology, and Human Values* 10, no. 52 (Summer 1985):8.

uative criteria. Further, such efforts should appreciate the complex pulls and pushes that the resulting diversity of evaluative modes exerts on the evaluation itself.

EVALUATIVE MODES

Roles are not the only factors that need to be distinguished in making sense of the criteria by which programs and policies can be critically appraised. Analysts have also found it useful to distinguish three general modes of evaluation. In the *outcome* mode, evaluation focuses on the outputs or outcomes of a particular activity. In the *input* mode, the emphasis is on the resources, skills, and people engaged in the activity. Finally, in the *process* mode, attention shifts to the methods used to transform political, economic, and other inputs into outputs/outcomes. Procedural rules that govern participation in and administration of the program are also relevant in this context. We next consider each of these modes separately, all the while keeping in mind that they are usually mingled in practical efforts to evaluate programs and policies.

Evaluation by outcomes or results is commonly viewed as the obvious way to assess the value of any purposive activity. Goals or benchmarks are defined, results are produced, and the two are compared. In the case of an educational program, for example, one would appraise the difference between pre- and post-tests, or between the experimental and the control group, on a number of different criteria. In health programs, the outcomes are changes in incidence and prevalence rates; in manpower programs, the outcomes are employment rates, and so on.

This mode of evaluation has a strong intuitive appeal. Indeed, one may well wonder why any other form of evaluation is at all needed. What common sense overlooks is that outcomes evaluation can be successfully performed only under rather stringent conditions. One obvious condition is that it must be possible to measure with reasonable precision the level and quality of the desired output or performance. If the indicator of performance is expressed by the distance between goals and outcomes, goals have to be clearly defined, outcomes must be unambiguously measurable, and the measuring instrument should be reliable.

These conditions are not often satisfied in practice, even approximately. When they are not, other modes of evaluation must be used. Evaluation by inputs focuses on the quantity and quality of the resources available to perform a certain task: number and technical quality of the staff, available information, level of funding, political support, and so on. These are indirect indicators of performance, at best. Unless a definite relationship between inputs and outputs or outcomes—a well-defined production function in the language of the economist—can be assumed, input variables are a poor proxy for what we are really interested in knowing, namely, how effective is a given program, or how good is a particular policy?

But in some situations, input variables are all the information the evaluator has to work with—for example, when the problem is to estimate the likely results of a new project or to assess the feasibility of a new program. Moreover, for purposes of control, input variables are often strategically more important than outputs. The detailed rules of public accounting that severely restrict the freedom of public managers to substitute one input for another in response to changing circumstances and new opportunities are a historically important example of evaluation and control by inputs.

Measurability is not the only, or the most serious, problem of outcomes evaluation. The main problem is that in many situations this type of evaluation gives policymakers, program managers, and interested citizens very little information upon which to act. Simply knowing that outcomes are satisfactory or unsatisfactory does not tell decision makers and critics very much about what to do. Where outcomes are evaluated without some reasonably accurate and coherent definition of the program, and without knowledge of the manner in which it is implemented, the results seldom provide a direction for action because the

decision maker lacks information about what produced the observed outcomes. Pure outcomes evaluation is the "black box"
approach to evaluation.[2]

Perhaps the best-known example of this approach are the
standardized achievement tests routinely administered in American public schools. Regarded by many evaluators as the epitome
of all that is most objective and "scientific" in educational evaluation, standardized tests are of little use to teachers and parents
and do not tell school officials what to do to improve the educational experience of students. In order to improve schools,
officials need information about what actually happens in the
classroom—course content, grading procedures, teaching methods, teacher-student interactions—and standardized tests do not
provide such information.[3]

Course content, grading procedures, teaching methods, and
teacher-student interactions are examples of process variables.
In many respects, process evaluation is the most subtle and in-
formative mode of evaluation—it provides information that input and output measures are almost sure to miss. Even in
commercial activities where outcomes can be easily quantified,
prudent managers try to avoid too narrow a focus on results.
They do so in the knowledge that the best outcome measures
never capture more than a small fraction of the total range of
performance that is important to the organization. For example,
sales volume is an unambiguous and robust output measure, but
it tends to focus too narrowly the attention of salespeople on
maximizing sales in the short run, with the result that they ignore
other functions that have a large effect on future sales. People
on straight commission have no incentive to arrange stocks, take
inventory, or train new salespeople who become their compet-
itors, and their supervisor cannot affect their salary by taking
into account the other, unmeasured goals.

Hence, as William G. Ouchi discovered in a study of seventy-
eight retail department store companies, commission payment

2. Michael Quinn Patton, *Utilization-Focused Evaluation* (Beverly Hills, Calif.:
Sage, 1978), 155–58.

3. Ibid., 155–57.

tends to be found in sales areas (like cosmetics, major appliances, and furniture) that require a relatively high degree of expertise and where therefore salespeople develop something like professional norms, or where knowledgeable and active clients can replace professional norms as another source of evaluation and control. Some companies even prohibit the maintenance of sales volume records for individual salespeople.[4]

EVALUATION AND CONTROL

Among the many possible purposes that evaluation may serve, directly or indirectly, control is certainly one of the most important. In fact, the relationship between evaluation and control is extremely close. On the one hand, in order to control any activity or organization, it is necessary to monitor and assess its performance with reference to a set of standards. On the other hand, evaluation modes and criteria have operational consequences for organizational and individual performance, since if people know that certain dimensions of performance are highly rated by the evaluators, they will tend to change their behavior accordingly.

Peter Blau, in his classic study of a public employment agency, provides instructive examples of the close relationship between performance and evaluative criteria. Thus, when the number of interviews completed by a subordinate was the only evidence the supervisor had for evaluating him, "the interviewer's interest in a good rating demanded that he maximize the number of interviews and therefore prohibited spending much time on locating jobs for clients. This rudimentary statistical record interfered with the agency's objective of finding jobs for clients in a period of job scarcity."[5] Even the more comprehensive system of monitoring introduced later produced serious displacements of organization goals:

4. "The Relationship between Organizational Structure and Organizational Control," *Administrative Science Quarterly* 22 (March 1977): 95–113.

5. *The Dynamics of Bureaucracy* (Chicago: University of Chicago Press, 1955, 38.

An instrument intended to further the achievement of organizational objectives, statistical records constrained interviewers to think of maximizing the indices as their major goal, sometimes at the expense of these very objectives. They avoided operations that would take up time without helping them to improve their record, such as interviewing clients for whom application forms had to be made out, and wasted their own and the public's time on activities intended only to raise the figures on their record. Their concentration on this goal, since it was important for their ratings, made them unresponsive to requests from clients that would interfere with its attainment. Preoccupation with productivity also affected the interpersonal relations among interviewers, and this constituted the most serious dysfunction of statistical reports.[6]

Similarly, there is evidence that compensating teachers on the basis of their output, as measured by student test score gains, creates incentives for teachers to concentrate their time on students in the middle of the test score distribution, neglecting those at the top who would advance well on their own and those at the botton whose test scores would not respond to small additional amounts of teacher time. Also, where the compensation of teachers depends on the number of students who acquire a set of narrowly defined skills (as, for example, under the payment-by-results plans used in England in the middle of the nineteenth century to compensate elementary school teachers), there is a tendency to narrow the curriculum to exclude all non-tested subjects—including many that are generally perceived to be important but are difficult to test.[7]

As these examples suggest, a careful analysis of the relevant production activity is essential for the choice of an appropriate method of evaluation and control, since knowledge of the activity provides the best clues to the responses that a particular mode of evaluation will elicit. More precisely, two parameters are crucial for determining the conditions under which different modes

6. Ibid., 46.
7. Richard J. Murnane and David K. Cohen, "Merit Pay and the Evaluation Problem: Why Most Merit Pay Plans Fail and a Few Survive," *Harvard Educational Review* 56, no. 1 (Feb. 1986): 1–17.

of evaluation/control are appropriate: measurability of the outcomes and knowledge of the process that generates the outcomes.[8] If, for the sake of simplicity, we dichotomize these parameters, we obtain the accompanying table:

KNOWLEDGE OF PROCESS

		Complete	Incomplete
MEASURABILITY OF OUTCOMES	High	Evaluation by process or by outcome	Evaluation by outcome
	Low	Evaluation by process	Evaluation by input

The four cells represent the situations in which the different modes of evaluation may be applied. The best situation is obviously when measurability of outcomes is high and the transformation process is completely known. Here the choice between process or outcomes evaluation depends on cost and economic convenience. Production of standardized goods using a well-understood technology is a familiar example. At the other extreme we find an activity like teaching whose outcome—education—is difficult to measure and where process is so idiosyncratic that it is impossible to characterize effective teaching as the consistent use of standardized techniques. Hence, teachers are evaluated mostly by input criteria like educational credentials and years of teaching experience, and this method of evaluation is reflected in uniform salary scales.

Activities that fall between these two extreme cases are usually evaluated by a mixture of the three basic methods. In for-profit firms, for example, managers are rewarded, at least in part, by results—sales and profits—but internal staff activities like research and development, accounting, or personnel management are evaluated by a combination of input and process criteria. On the other hand, traditional methods of evaluation and control of public programs rely heavily on inputs, but some analysts

8. Ouchi, "Organizational Structure and Organizational Control," 97–99.

think that recent advances in the measurement of outcomes in areas like health care and personal social services may eventually induce a shift in policy concern from inputs to outcomes. If true, this development would have important consequences for public accountability.

ACCOUNTABILITY

Our discussion of different roles and modes of evaluation, and of the relationship between evaluation and control, bears directly on the problem of public accountability. In a democracy managers and producers of public services are expected to be accountable for their performance to those who consume their services and to those who pay for them, or to their political representatives. Accountability cannot be enforced without adequate standards of performance, but these, as we have seen, are often difficult to define. Traditional input criteria like budgetary rules, administrative guidelines, or staffing ratios may be sufficient for purposes of oversight, but cannot satisfy the growing demand to state accountability in terms of outputs and to reward those who produce more efficiently.

The advocates of accountability by results argue that public managers should be free to choose the way they allocate their resources as long as they achieve specific targets. This procedure would free them from cumbersome and ineffective input controls and provide powerful incentives to improve results, just as private managers are free to vary production methods but are rewarded according to sales and profits.

Like outcomes evaluation, the idea of accountability by results has a strong intuitive appeal. It sounds simple and reasonable; implementing it, however, is hard. The congenital reluctance of liberal democracies to grant too much discretion to public administrators is only part of the problem. Another and more immediate reason for the difficulty of implementing the idea is that most public programs have vague and diverse goals, and as a consequence agreement about relevant criteria of success is hard to achieve.

The exact nature of the difficulty is not always clearly under-stood. For example, some analysts claim that it is possible today to develop the objective measures of performance that are needed to implement the concept of accountability by results. A. J. Culyer, a British economist, has recently written that "in health care, education and the personal social services it is now feasible to measure and monitor outcome. For example, we can measure health. We can measure dependency of the young and the old. We can measure handicap. We can measure deprivation. We can measure attainment of educational and social skills. We can associate changes in these measures with the forms of care we provide."[9] The availability of such measures, Culyer argues, represents a major, indeed a revolutionary change in the way we manage and finance social services and the way we expect the professionals who provide them to be accountable to society as a whole.

But what does measurability mean in the present context? With sufficient ingenuity it is always possible to devise scalar measures of particular dimensions of performance. The goals of most public programs, however, are multidimensional. Schools, for example, are supposed to improve cognitive skills, but also to socialize young children and teach them democratic values. Hence, multiple measures are needed to reflect multiple objectives and to avoid distorting performance.

Even if one assumes that the level of achievement of each separate objective could be measured unambiguously and ob-jectively, one would still have to solve the problem of aggrega-tion, that is, of reaching a consensus about the weights to be assigned to the various objectives. Until a consensus is reached, there is no overall measure of performance. Disagreement about the weights is to be expected, however, since the issue of weights is at its core a debate about how the activity should be organized and whose interests matter the most.

Moreover, we know that performance in the public sector can seldom be expressed by means of output measures alone. In

9. *The Withering of the Welfare State? Whither the Welfare State?* (Vancouver: Department of Economics, University of British Columbia, 1986), 25.

general, a combination of input, process, and output criteria is needed, and different groups will also disagree about the weights to be assigned to the different elements of the combination. In education, for example, teachers' unions favor input criteria like years of teaching experience, size of classes, and hours of work, while parents are more concerned with various dimensions of outcome and process.

Because the issue of weights is so divisive, most policy debates about health, education, or social services avoid the problem. Instead of openly debating what the weights should be, the tendency is to delegate decisions about resource allocation to the service producers. But such delegation is not consistent with the idea of accountability by results, for the different decisions about weights of individual producers mean that they are each trying to produce a somewhat different mix of outputs.[10] The need, then, is less to develop "objective" measures of outcomes (though improved measurement would certainly help) than to begin and sustain a wide-ranging dialogue about the meaning and implication of different sets of weights among producers and users of public services.

The difficulties of evaluation by results loom even larger in debates about the accountability of government to the legislature and the electorate. In the past it may have been possible to agree on a few stable standards—maintaining law and order and a stable currency at home, peace abroad—for evaluating the activities of government. But with the great expansion of these activities and the lengthening of the time span on which informed judgments of performance should be based, the record of any government is much less clear and the evaluative criteria are correspondingly more controversial.[11]

Under such conditions, the confidence that accountability is supposed to generate can hardly depend on the relation between some measurable outcome and a predetermined standard of success. Rather, it depends on methods of evaluation capable of

10. Murnane and Cohen, "Merit Pay and the Evaluation Problem," 5.

11. Geoffrey Vickers, *The Art of Judgment* (London: Chapman and Hall, 1965), 149.

providing more information than a simple judgment of success or failure. Exclusive reliance on measures of short-term results often leads to the conclusion that most public policies are ineffective. The apparently ubiquitous phenomenon of "little effect" concerns professional evaluators. As Carol Weiss writes, one of the major obstacles to putting evaluation results to use is precisely their dismaying tendency to show that the program has had little effect.[12] Organizations do not fare better: "Measured against the Olympic heights of the goal, most organizations score the same— very low effectiveness. The differences among organizations are of little significance."[13] Programs and organizations, like scientific theories, seem to be born to be refuted, and evaluation, as usually conceived and practiced, can play no crucial role in their development.

The phenomenon of "little effect" becomes less surprising once we recognize that evaluation exclusively in terms of short-term results is bound to be inconclusive under normal circumstances. First, to get on with their work, evaluators must assume that their models and measuring techniques are unproblematic, or at least less problematic than the working hypotheses incorporated in the program they evaluate. In fact, a conclusion of little or no effect could be interpreted as a failure of the evaluator's model just as well as a failure of the program.

Second, any reasonably accurate and coherent description of a particular program must take into consideration the policy framework in which the program is embedded. In particular, its position with respect to the policy core is likely to influence in a significant way how the program is implemented, the level of support it enjoys, and the meaning it has for different policy actors. Even the most sophisticated measures of outputs/outcomes are almost sure to miss these aspects of the program and thus may underestimate its effects.

Finally, in evaluating efforts to significantly change the be-

12. "Evaluation Research in the Political Context," in E. L. Struening and M. Guttentag, eds., *Handbook of Evaluation Research*, vol. 2 (London: Sage, 1975), 13–25.

13. Amitai Etzioni, "Two Approaches to Organizational Analysis: A Critique and a Suggestion," *Administrative Science Quarterly* 5, no. 2 (1960): 258.

havior of large numbers of people, a limited time frame is inappropriate because it neglects both the severity of the initial administrative problems and the possibility of learning by doing. For example, in the case of compensatory education under Title I of the U.S. Elementary and Secondary Education Act, evaluation studies conducted a few years after passage of the 1965 legislation produced widespread evidence that disadvantaged students were showing no improvement in basic learning skills. Yet studies conducted after a decade of implementation revealed significant improvements in the administration of the program and a number of substantial improvements in educational performances. The new findings suggest that there was a pattern of learning by program administrators and their congressional supporters as they identified obstacles and then devised various strategies to deal with them.[14]

To sum up, the greatest problems of public accountability and policy evaluation are associated with the choice of criteria by which to measure success. Experts and citizens alike must face the inevitable conflict between crude but intuitively appealing criteria on the one hand, and more refined but also more controversial criteria on the other. This conflict may not have been so serious once. As Geoffrey Vickers has observed, there have been times in the not-so-distant past when popular expectations were relatively clear, realistic and verifiable—the maintenance of law and order, protection against foreign aggression, a stable currency, a stable level of taxation, relief of extreme poverty. Today we expect much more from our government, but we do not know precisely how *any* government could fulfill our expectations.

At the same time, change—largely self-induced, as we saw in the last chapter—has become so rapid that the past becomes an ever less reliable guide to the future. Thus, policy outcomes become increasingly elusive both because we are less certain about the limits of the possible in public policy and because we

14. Paul A. Sabatier, "What Can We Learn from Implementation Research?", in Franz-Xavier Kaufmann, Giandomenico Majone, and Vincent Ostrom, eds., *Guidance, Control, and Evaluation in the Public Sector* (Berlin: Walter de Gruyter, 1986), 313–26.

suspect that the most important results may not yet have had time to appear. In these conditions the mere comparison of immediate results with expectations is likely to be uninformative as well as inconclusive.

According to social psychologists, learning is the dominant form in which rationality exhibits itself in situations of great cognitive complexity. This suggests that the rationality of public policy-making depends more on improving the learning capacity of the various organs of public deliberation than on maximizing achievement of particular goals.

It is not the task of analysts to resolve fundamental disagreements about evaluative criteria and standards of accountability; only the political process can do that. However, analysts can contribute to societal learning by refining the standards of appraisal of public programs and by encouraging a more sophisticated understanding of public policies than is possible from a single perspective. The need today is less to develop "objective" measures of outcomes—the traditional aim of evaluation research—than to facilitate a wide-ranging dialogue among advocates of different criteria.

Index